Romanticism

Author: Léon Rosenthal
Translator: Bérengère Mauduit

Layout:
BASELINE CO LTD
33 Ter – 33 Bis Mac Dinh Chi St.,
Star Building; 6th Floor
District 1, Ho Chi Minh City
Vietnam

© 2008, Parsktone Press International, New York, USA
© 2008, Confidential Concepts, worldwide, USA

ISBN 978-1-84484-458-6

Printed in China

Léon Rosenthal

Romanticism

PARKSTONE
INTERNATIONAL

– Contents –

I. The Precursors of Romanticism

The Romantic Age! Youth, ardour, a generous faith in art, excessive passions; amongst fevers, exaggerations, errors, it was a period really full of ideas, personalities and works.

Literary Romanticism has been subject to great arguments and violent controversy, particularly because it was considered to be responsible for divisive religious, political or social tendencies. Romantic art received less attention, perhaps because it seemed comparatively unimportant. However, it is possible to dissociate the two movements. They were linked not because of personal friendships developing by chance between a few painters and writers but because those movements, in their different ways, share in the same origin. Born from a common mindset, they had developed in the same atmosphere. There was a Romantic generation the members of which applied their minds to literature and the arts as well as to science, philosophy, politics or industry – in fact to all the forms of activity to which their minds could possibly be applied.

The canons of Romanticism were first formulated in Germany at the end of the eighteenth century. As early as 1770 and 1780 representatives of *Sturm und Drang*, a movement both literary and political, meaning literally 'storm and stress', were rebelling against the Enlightenment and its values. Friedrich von Schiller and Johann Wolfgang von Goethe were amongst the followers of *Sturm und Drang*, who made a religion of individualism and nature as advocated by Jean-Jacques Rousseau in the middle of the eighteenth century. However, despite that wave of protest the rejection of classical rules was only partial. *Sturm und Drang* turned its back on classical traditions and literary conventions but its canons of beauty were still based on Antiquity and prescribed the perfection and harmony of forms. Classicism was totally rejected as a whole by the intellectuals contributing to the journal *Athenaeum*, amongst whom were Wilhelm von Schelling and Novalis representing the 'Iena Romantics' group. In contrast with earlier values they put an emphasis on the feeling of infinity, mysticism and the expression of irrationality.

In Ireland, the *Philosophical Enquiry into the Origin of our Ideas of the Sublime and the Beautiful* by Edmund Burke, published in 1756, developed the Romantic vision of nature. In Burke's remarks on painting, one notes the same tendency through "the painting of the sublime" on the one hand and the "mysticism of landscapes" on the other, clearly exemplified by the works of Caspar David Friedrich. In 1762, James McPherson's English translation of *Poems of Ossian* became a reference for Romanticism. Allegedly attributed to a Scottish bard of the third century, the origins of the book are mysterious but it appealed to the collective imagination and plunged its readers into the depths of their dreams.

Thus the European literature of the eighteenth century paved the way for Romanticism, but it is in the art of the nineteenth century, particularly in France, that it reached its zenith. French

Philipp Otto Runge,
The Lesson of the Nightingale,
1804-1805.
Oil on canvas, 104.7 x 88.5 cm.
Hamburger Kunsthalle, Hamburg.

art at the time formed an imposing structure whose magnificent order reflected the heroic times that had built it. A fanatical admiration for Graeco-Roman Antiquity was still defended. Art's only goal seemed to be to revive the inspiration and methods of that blessed time, which alone had managed to bring pure, serene and ideal beauty out of humanity. But Antiquity could appear multi-faced depending on the eyes and predispositions of its admirers: by turn it could be solemn, pleasant, frivolous, noble, generous or depraved. When men imagined it tense, stiff, stilted and raised towards inaccessible peaks they projected their own genius onto it. Through Socrates, Romulus and Leonidas they glorified their own century. They praised the human figure, powerful bodies with wide chests, regular facial features, strong contours, refined drawing, vivid colours devoid of ornaments, subordinated nature reduced to the passive role of décor. Everything echoed the tendencies of generations galvanised first by their passion for freedom and then for glory. Bare and stilted statues, devoid of accentuation, appealed to eyes that could not stand the graces of the eighteenth century. Palaces, temples and commemorative monuments tried to convey the majesty of that time through plain, solid and large structures drawing on Vitruve's repertoire. Inside the buildings, mahogany furniture followed heavy architectural patterns and decorations included chiselled noble copperware, solemn chandeliers and grandfather clocks, wall coverings adorned with large geometrical patterns in which gold, green and Etruscan red were associated, composed austere and simple harmonies designed for a new and rather unrefined society that had forgotten the gentle way of life. It was an artificial but perfectly adequate setting whose consistency was quite remarkable and particularly striking when contrasted with the disorder of the following period. The brilliance of that style, though it was soon to be tarnished, was nevertheless magnificent. At the same time that France provided politics, sciences and the army with men of genius or great talent, she also supplied the arts with an élite, a whole host of stars.

If we put aside our modern prejudices we can understand the pride with which people of the time talked of the "French School". Around David, the leader, there were painters like Girodet, Gérard, Guérin, Gros and Proudhon. Most of these masters were still active when the Empire collapsed, and they had trained students whose works had started to appear. Based on a strong doctrine illustrated by exemplary works, the French School was well on course to carry on its glorious career.

However, it was fragile as was the Empire itself and complex forces were at work to try and destroy it despite its triumphant appearances. Strangely enough, the French School imposed a precise discipline on artists at the very time when the Revolution was breaking the social codes and teaching individuals that their originality, boldness and energy could get them where they wanted in society. In some it shook up instincts of generosity that had been put to sleep by systematic minds; to others, who had been repressing desires of wealth, pleasure and brilliance, it offered a multitude of exciting opportunities and made them seek new and diverse acquaintances and lifestyles. Hypnotised by a conventional view of Antiquity, David had ignored the past totally until the revolutionary crisis rekindled his interest in history. As a child Michelet, wild with enthusiasm, would pace up and down the rooms of the Musée des Monuments Français (Museum of French Monuments) where

Jean-Auguste-Dominique Ingres,
The Vow of Louis XIII, 1824.
Oil on canvas, 421 x 262 cm.
Cathédrale Notre-Dame, Montauban.

VIRG. DEI P.
REGN. VOV
LUDOV. XIII
A.R.S.H
MDCXXXVIII
FEB.

Lenoir, who founded the museum with the stone works he saved from the violent fury of the Revolution, displayed several centuries of history. A certain image of France started to be outlined, albeit vague and pale at first, and the troubadour style foreshadowed the development of a new kind of spirit.

At the same time there arose an interest in churches and cathedrals, buildings which had been previously looked down upon. In 1802 Chateaubriand published *Genius of Christianity* which echoed the hopes of a whole generation. He claimed in it that religious inspiration was superior to all others. Elsewhere, the Empire kept silent whilst economic activity slowed down and young men were decimated in a state permanently at war, which caused a feeling of weariness. The influence of Rousseau deepened in this climate, manifest in Sénancour's 1804 telling of *Obermann's* dark destiny, who alone in the Alps sought consolation in nature.

So despite appearing arrogant the general atmosphere tended towards the dissolution of the French School. But it faced more direct assaults from within the artistic world itself. David had established himself through total rebellion against the eighteenth century. He disowned his masters and, with them, the whole inheritance of traditions accumulated since the Renaissance, preferring antique style models and casting. In 1793 the Louvre Museum opened to the public. Victories over Italy and Flanders allowed it soon to be filled with masterpieces whilst a growing fancy of collectors for Dutch paintings became quite noticeable.

At the heart of the French School, amongst its protagonists and most famous masters, a new and transformed future was in preparation, and the people of the time got a partial sense of it. They did not realise that *The Death of Marat, The Coronation* or the multiplication of portraits helped artists in liberating themselves, but they feared Gros's action. A shy man, whose most sincere desire would have been to become the loyal right-hand man of David, he was driven by an internal force seemingly in spite of himself. Unwillingly, he carried the truths that were about to blossom. *Napoleon at Jaffa* was more than the preface to Romanticism. It asserted the joy of painting as well as a research into characterisation, movement and liveliness, to which orientalism and a picturesque quality were added. This famous painting that young people kept referring to was not an exceptional phenomenon, however. The whole of Gros's work, his huge paintings, his portraits, sketches and watercolours, developed a whole programme: the supremacy of colour, the study of places and races, an interest in animals and particularly the big cats. National history was represented by the *Visit of Charles V and François I at Saint-Denis*; he thought of *Othello* and *Ugolin* in 1804 and the posthumous portrait of Lucien Bonaparte's wife is shrouded in a modern kind of melancholy.

Ingres's works like *Jupiter and Thetis* – still amazing to us nowadays – were painted at the time of David's supremacy and are full of inspiration, sensitivity and expressive moods that were totally new. Among so many docile artists Ingres showed an untameable independence; he had broken off with David and wanted to 'become an innovator, have his works imprinted with a character unknown' before him. Acquaintance with the Italian primitives had polished his subtle drawing. He was one of the first to acknowledge their art as he was also the first to consider Greek vases. He would feed his genius with ideas from all sorts of areas: classical Antiquity, history, poetry, the reality of the time and oriental countries. He did not look

Jean-Baptiste Mallet,
Gothic Bathroom, 1810.
Oil on canvas, 40.5 x 32.5 cm.
Château-Musée de Dieppe, Dieppe.

Hubert Robert,
Design for the Grande Galerie in the Louvre, 1796.
Oil on canvas, 115 x 145 cm.
Musée du Louvre, Paris.

down on colour, adored Titian and, being versatile, nervous, changing his style from one painting to the other, he would sometimes invent sharp harmonies and precious dissonances. With an implacable precision but also infinite suppleness his lines shrouded pure but non abstract shapes in which concentrated fieriness and a sensual love for beauty were visible. He who painted Fingal's fantasy paradise, Thetis' wavy body, and surrounded the dreamy Madame de Sénones with a floating languid atmosphere was a pre-Romantic in his own way, like Gros, and in fact more exceptional and more modern than the latter. His power was not yet recognised, though. People were sensitive to a charm that was seen as ineffable but feared the technical examples that he set. It was believed that he drew badly because he was not superstitious about the outline. On bluish paper he would use charcoal and chalk to bring out volumes and shroud synthetic and quivering shapes in space. He kept a love for graces in an heroic age but with a penetrating fieriness unknown to the eighteenth century, and he added a sense of worry to it that dragged him away from the past and made him closer to us.

Sculpture developed in a more balanced way. It was obsessed by a passion for heroic ideals more than any other form of art. Houdon continued to flourish, restating his profound genius with a bust of Napoleon.

A few signs of something about to be born were also visible in architecture. The emperor's official architects, Percier and Fontaine, were touched by the smiles of the Italian Renaissance.

So at a time when it was believed that the arts had taken a definite direction and found fixed shapes, some forces were at work preparing for an evolution that was waiting to happen. Those forces were complex and paradoxical in many ways. Some wished for the supremacy of reality whilst others praised imagination and dreams. None of these tendencies gave way but their fate would be determined by future events. If the Empire had grown stronger and had settled in a stable order, minds would have relaxed gradually; a calm, healthy and balanced kind of art would probably have developed ensuring the triumph of realism. But on the contrary, if a storm was to burst out, a period of crisis would consequently start in which disoriented artists would listen to their sensitivity and nerves rather than rationality: that would mark the triumph of Romanticism.

It turned out to be a storm and a most terrible one. The fall of the Empire, the invasion of the country and the return of the Bourbons shook France deeply, and it was left feeling humiliated and hurt. From then on, neither religion, politics nor any position in society could offer a secure shelter. The *mal du siècle* became exacerbated. Helpless men turned in on themselves; they looked into their own minds in search of the laws at work behind their actions. They soared painfully on the uncertain paths of liberty, guided by their feelings and not by logic. At that time England, from which France had been cut off because of war, recreated the contacts initiated by Voltaire in the eighteenth century. France had already turned to Germany, and the influence of Germanic countries occurred precisely in the way that Madame de Staël had indicated with great lucidity: Goethe, Schiller, Shakespeare, Walter Scott, Constable, Lawrence and Beethoven came to feed the longings of an anxious generation. This is how Romantic times started.

Édouard Cibot,
Anne Boleyn in the Tower, 1835.
Oil on canvas, 162 x 129 cm.
Musée Rolin, Autun.

Anne-Louis Girodet de Roucy,
called **Girodet-Trioson,**
The Entombment of Atala, 1808.
Oil on canvas, 207 x 267 cm.
Musée du Louvre, Paris.

J'AI PASSÉ COMME
LA FLEUR

J'AI SECHÉ COMME L'HERBE
DES CHAMPS

II. The Romantic Period

At the Exhibition of 1817, the first to take place after the Restoration, the public did not notice any signs of change. Despite David's exile, the same masters were present defending the same ideas. Beside them there were some young people, their students and followers, supporting the cause.

No doubt it was wished that politics had not imposed or suggested topics remote from the artistic mission such as historical anecdotes or religious themes. Gérard had painted the *Entry of Henri IV into Paris* in the same way that he had celebrated the *10th August* in the past. There were also signs of weariness; with shy audacity some artists had created scenes with a dramatic quality or tinged with light effects. In fact, there was nothing there to write home about. The young Horace Vernet displayed a large picturesque painting with his *Battle of Las Navas de Tolosa* but that was an isolated case; the *Grand Condé* by David d'Angers triggered some curiosity but without raising fears.

However, fervent, anxious and nervous young people questioned and looked for the future in studios or at the Louvre at that very time. They sensed, without understanding the exact reasons for it, that life was now to be found outside the formulae that had ensured the glory of French art for half a century. There had been a soul lying in these tried and tested formulae which was no longer shared by these young people. Some historic and respectable academic rules were still in use, but outdated. Famous professors no longer had control over these young people. They fumbled for new means of expression or, as sometimes happens in such situations, they would temporarily seek guidance from a friend who seemed momentarily inspired.

At the Exhibition of 1819 latent ideas suddenly appeared, revealing themselves in the scandal of *The Raft of the Medusa*. It was a huge painting whose dimensions alone were a challenge, and it imposed authority in itself even upon those who were distressed by it. No doubt that the battle had started. In that painting, Géricault rejected everything that the French School had stood for: the hierarchy of genres (as he treated a news item like an epic), ideal beauty, the supremacy of drawing, apparent finish, balanced order and serenity.

That vehemently powerful work claimed the joy of painting, the rights of movement, drama, and life. Beyond David's canon, it was based on principles from the past and strengthened by the tradition it had returned to, whilst at the same time announcing a free form of art. Critics moaned and were disturbed by the multiplication of mundane and religious topics, but young people praised Géricault and saw in him their new leader. He still had a natural penchant for the realist epic that few shared, but he set an example for all and gave them the courage to assert themselves.

Those around him, and in particular the young Delacroix, were attracted by his work and could see something special in it. His drawings, gouaches and watercolours often confirmed

Eugène Delacroix,
*Liberty Leading the People
(28th July 1830),* 1830.
Oil on canvas, 260 x 325 cm.
Musée du Louvre, Paris.

what Gros had intuitively discovered, but at the same time he pioneered techniques in different fields. Invented in 1796, lithography had only produced uncertain and imperfect outcomes; Géricault took it up and, with remarkable confidence, revealed its full potential. Lithography would have been inadequate for David and his students, who would have found it too greasy, supple, colourful and sometimes excessive, but it turned out to be perfectly suitable for the new generation.

Géricault's action was profound and long lasting though he did not show work in public again after the *Medusa*. He did not take part in the Exhibition of 1822 and died at the beginning of 1824. Before Géricault's death, Eugène Delacroix had taken up his torch. *Dante and Virgil* was showed at the Exhibition of 1822 and made him famous. Close to him were artists like Bonington, Champmartin, Sigalon, Camille Roqueplan, Ary Scheffer and Achille Devéria, some of whom achieved enduring fame.

At the Exhibition of 1824 scattered signs of change had turned into a generalised movement in which was at stake the whole direction that art was to take. The Romantics flocked together. Besides Bonington, Copley Fielding, Constable and Lawrence came to display their works at the Exhibition as if they wanted to support the *avant-garde*.

Facing such attacks and desertion, the French School resisted; it would not let go and the fight turned out to be much harder for artists than writers. Victor Hugo and his emulators faced mediocre writers with worn out, passé formulae who opposed them with insults and mockery but not with powerful works. However, the School which the young artists had decided to destroy was too recent, and the fits of enthusiasm that it had produced were only just past. Girodet was still very successful with *Pygmalion* at the Exhibition of 1819, but time was not on the School's side and nobody had David's authority or the productivity needed either to impose discipline on the young or to stimulate them and give them confidence in proven doctrines. A figure to lead the resistance was looked for, and Ingres was called on for help.

At the time he was blacklisted. *La Grande Odalisque*, on display beside *Roger delivering Angelica* at the Exhibition of 1819, had been accused of multiple flaws and seen as directing art backwards to its primitive age, though avant-garde artists appreciated his work. At the Exhibition of 1824, however, *The Vow of Louis XIII* created a sudden reversal of the situation and put him back in favour with the orthodox point of view.

He was seen as the saviour who was needed: the idiosyncratic features of his genius were ignored whilst his science and energy were put at the forefront. In 1825 he was elected a member of the *Institut*.

In 1825 Charles X was crowned in Reims. Gothic decoration was chosen for the ceremony: there was a gallery in front of the façade as well as inside the nave. These solemn circumstances helped assert the triumph of the Middle Ages that had been so looked down on. Everything worked in favour of this reversal: it was in the interest of religion and politics whilst being also supported by the development of historic sciences. In 1831 the novel *Notre-Dame de Paris* made the craze for medievalism reach its peak. It was visible everywhere, in the inspiration of artists and writers, trinkets, furniture and fashion.

Antoine Jean Gros and **Auguste Deaby**, *The Battle of the Pyramids (21st July 1798)*, first quarter of the 19th century. Oil on canvas, 389 x 511 cm. Musée national du château et des Trianons, Versailles.

David's death in Brussels at the beginning of 1826 went almost unnoticed. A few weeks later an exhibition of Greek art was held. Some of the School's most famous paintings were displayed, besides which Delacroix, Devéria, Roqueplan and Scheffer also exhibited their work. The stylistic confrontation had exactly the effect that could have been expected: faded enthusiasms were revived and avant-garde artists were crushed by the weight of the glorious past. However, all was in vain and the dying body could not be brought back to life. Nevertheless, the Romantics lost some support, and from then on they were attacked mercilessly.

1827 was marked by the preface to *Cromwell*. The parallel between Hugo and Delacroix, which was to become famous, was first made by Louis Vitet in the *Globe*. The artistic struggle reached its peak, and the Exhibition of 1827 turned into a 'convention on painting', as a contemporary put it. Delacroix's *Sardanapale*, Devéria's *Birth of Henri IV*, and Ary Scheffer's *Souliot Women* were to be seen. Opposite that group there were *The Death of Elisabeth* and *The Taking of the Trocadero* by Paul Delaroche, *Mazeppa* by Horace Vernet, and *Torquato Tasso* by Robert Fleury. Bonington displayed *The View of Venice* and Lawrence *Master Lambton*. Such a list gives testimony to an exceptional creative intensity. Inspired, feverish, solid or skilful; how could those paintings not trouble minds? Sigalon failed totally. So did Delacroix, whose *Marin Faliero* did not raise any interest whilst *Sardanapale* was slated equally by his friends and enemies. It was a success for Boulanger and a short-lived triumph for the creator of *The Birth of Henri IV*, Eugène Devéria, of whom it was briefly thought that he might become the leader of the Romantics. Two beginners, Corot and Paul Huet, were hardly noticed in the turmoil yet it was through them that landscapes would be included in the controversy.

A few days after the Exhibition started some new rooms opened at the Louvre. On one of the ceilings Ingres had painted The *Apotheosis of Homer*. To tell the truth, no-one understood it, and it prompted mostly the admiration of the Romantics.

The first performance of the play *Henri III and his Court* by Alexandre Dumas on 10 February 1829 was not solely a literary event. It revealed some deep changes in the performing arts. Doric porticos which could hardly fill the stage were no longer fashionable; staging, décor and costumes grew richer and were enlivened by Romantic inspiration.

The opening of the Conservatoire's concerts by Habeneck in 1828 allowed music lovers to discover and develop the cult of Beethoven. Around the end of 1830, Berlioz conducted his *Symphonie fantastique*. He transferred into the realm of music the same enthusiasm and rage that was going on in painting and poetry, and thus found himself, like Victor Hugo or Delacroix, a key figure in the avant-garde.

The revolution had just begun. It created generous exaltation and a lot of hope. It seemed that the France which had been humiliated under the Restoration regime was about to be reborn. *Freedom guiding the People* by Delacroix was the sign of that *élan*. Had it endured, the direction taken by the arts would have been substantially different. Reconciled with their time and bathed in civic spirit, artists would have forgotten their reveries and feverish feelings and would have been reconnected to reality. The Monarchie de Juillet

Joseph Mallord William Turner,
The Field of Waterloo, 1818.
Oil on canvas, 147.3 x 238.8 cm.
Tate Gallery, London.

23

dispelled illusions born on the barricades almost immediately. Artists turned back to the silence of their studios.

Yet the new regime provided fighters in unexpected fields of activity. Political caricature sprang up with an incredible violence and fierceness but also unbelievable artistic brilliance. Decamps, Raffet and Grandville opened the way to Daumier, and when the laws of September 1834 stopped their sarcasm against Louis-Philippe their satirical wittiness started targeting public mores, and Gavarni applied his sharp mind with endless resourcefulness.

Around that time David's school seemed utterly exhausted. Gros's suicide, after the bad reception of his works at the 1835 Exhibition had driven him to despair, could be perceived as a token gesture. Of course that did not prevent followers of David from going on with their teaching, keeping their seats at the *Institut,* and providing an increased number of

bloodless, conventional and outrageous paintings to decorate the monuments and churches of Paris in particular. The *Institut*, that had the juries of exhibitions under its control, proscribed people like Delacroix, Decamps, Chassériau and, above all, landscape painters throughout the Monarchie de Juillet.

Delacroix was fully accomplished by then. He painted the admirable *Algiers Women* in 1834, *Saint Sebastian* in 1836, *Medea* and *Taillebourg* in 1838, *Trajan* and *The Shipwreck of Don Juan* in 1840, The *Crusaders of Constantinople* in 1841 and *Marcus Aurelius* in 1845. Decamps created high quality works with the same regularity. Chassériau, a child prodigy brought up in Ingres's studio, asked the Romantics to help him express his refined and complex desires. In his famous lessons on colour, Chevreul justified Delacroix's technical intuitions and drew up new laws that could allow daring ideas to develop.

Francisco de Goya y Lucientes,
The Third of May, 1808: The Execution of the Defenders of Madrid, 1814.
Oil on canvas, 268 x 347 cm.
Museo Nacional del Prado, Madrid.

Revolution had expanded everywhere. Landscape painting was bubbling with excitement. An imposing group made up of Paul Huet, Dupré, Théodore Rousseau, Daubigny and Corot offered original ways of feeling and representing natural landscapes. At the Exhibition of 1827, *Mercury* by Rude foreshadowed a renewal in sculpture stamped with authority. Turmoil reached sculpture too. David d'Angers modelled statues, busts and medallions of his most famous contemporaries and sculpted the pediment of the Panthéon in 1837. On the Arc de Triomphe, Rude celebrated the *Departure* of the revolutionary armies with epic grandeur and Barye managed to catch and represent the lively ferocity of the great cats.

Parallel to that, a craze for images developed and lithography played a central role. Illustrations started to appear everywhere in books. Whilst the monumental publication of the *Voyages pittoresques et romantiques dans l'ancienne France* was going on, enriched by lithographs, some of the most beautiful of which were carried out by Bonington and Isabey, books of all kinds were adorned with frontispieces, images, lithographs, etchings and steel engravings. With the help of incredibly skilful craftsmen, wood allowed illustrations of perfect typographic quality to be inserted in the text. The *Magasin pittoresque* relied heavily on images in its effort at encyclopaedic popularisation.

Deep changes were also visible in furniture, interior design, clothing and even hairdressing: tasteful or not, art was taken into consideration in all areas. Collectors gathered marvels from the past and threw new light upon them. The choice of a jacket or haircut or the growth of a beard showed aesthetic beliefs and were perceived as manifestos. Without knowing it, elegant men and ladies going to the opera disguised as transvestites, slovenly-dressed young people complaining about the fuss ordered by Chicard, all took up the style established by the Duchess of Berry and Alexandre Dumas. Unexpected costumes, unreliable archaeological extravaganzas, plastic surprises, medleys of colour and flashiness, all were a visual feast added to music or dance.

Was the whole movement a hundred per cent Romantic? Undoubtedly analysis reveals that some aspects were not a matter for Romanticism but parodies, imitations and compromises would not have happened if some active and vivid ferment had not been at work, modelling the period, and people of the time, whether scandalised or overjoyed, saw Romanticism everywhere.

Indeed, Romanticism had swept across the whole of society. Yet, at the same time that one could see signs of it everywhere, it was already deeply eroded and going into decline.

Just after the first battles, Romanticism faced some opposition in the public which it was not going to overcome. I am not referring here to the surprise that Romantic works caused, for every new form of art requires some time for the public to adapt, become educated and eventually understand it. It is also obvious that the eccentric side of early Romanticism would only raise momentary curiosity. No, the essence of Romanticism itself was repugnant to the spirit in general, and the French spirit in particular.

With traditions of clarity, order, logic and analysis and the pre-eminence of rational thinking, everything in France was against an aesthetic movement which praised feeling

Francesco Podesti,
Henry II, King of France, Mortally Wounded in a Joust, Blessing the Marriage of his Sister Marguerite de Valois with Emmanuel-Philibert de Savoie, 1844.
Oil on canvas, 178 x 280 cm.
Castello ducale, Agliè.

and passion and relied on the soul's intimate forces instead of asking for well thought out adhesion.

Romantic success was never total and the more characteristic the works, the more the polemic reactions they caused. Year after year the general atmosphere was less and less in the Romantics' favour. Besides, material wealth softened the *mal du siècle.* When time came for minds to be taken over by new passions, social and humanitarian tendencies as well as political claims called for action, and focused everybody's attention on the realities of the time, preparing for new artistic ideals.

The defection of artists themselves was a serious sign of the movement running out of steam. Louis Boulanger, for whom Hugo cherished great hopes and whose zeal had led him to truly extravagant behaviour, finally turned to dull and spineless painting. Overwhelmed by the weight of early glory, and despite a few successful comebacks, Eugène Devéria disappeared too. Ary Scheffer turned his back on the colourfulness of *Gaston of Foix* and preferred pale philosophical abstraction.

Others looked only for success and, in order to achieve it, they weakened their effects, added mannerism and, in the end, produced watered-down Romanticism. Some tried to revive the graces of the eighteenth century that they had talked down in the past. Achille Devéria and Célestin Nanteuil came down with a bump and produced undemanding lithographs.

The crowd seemed to prefer skilful men who produced mundane or dramatic images using a plain language devoid of technical originality. Avatars, weaknesses of disoriented artists and an uneducated public all had a negative impact but then an even more damaging phenomenon occurred. From 1840 on, the suppressed classical tendencies found a new vigour and claimed revenge; public opinion called for a reaction and young people turned away from Romanticism. Victor Hugo's play *The Burgraves* was a memorable failure, and Ingres suddenly appeared like the hero of the hour. He was just back from Italy, where he had managed the Ecole de Rome and had had an incredible influence on his pupils. He had just painted the *Stratonice*, which was showered with praise. He was acclaimed as a saviour

Francisco de Goya y Lucientes,
Charles IV and his Family, c. 1800.
Oil on canvas, 280 x 336 cm.
Museo Nacional del Prado, Madrid.

and humbly agreed to stand up in the sacred cause of art. He had soon forgotten his previous ambitions and with total authority he proclaimed the cult of the beautiful and condemned any deviation from the rule. He had only a few direct disciples but, nevertheless, dull and faded paintings reappeared everywhere. Neo-classical landscape painters turned to Antiquity again and were influenced by Poussin. The general appearance of exhibitions changed completely: colour, movement and life disappeared. Romantic art was still allowed in, but seemed out of place. Greyness and a sense of wisdom had swept in. An English man felt like going for a cold bath as he entered the Exhibition of 1846. New artists appeared like Gérôme with his *Cockfighting*; the calculated and glamorous effects of the *Decadent Romans* by Couture appeared vivid and inspired.

It was a time of helplessness. Hyperbolic assertions, polemic beliefs and basic negation were not worthwhile anymore. Either out of scepticism or indifference the most sensitive people accepted the novelties that stood out, whatever doctrine they stemmed from. They preached eclecticism, and events seemed to prove them right. Times were weary though each year probably had its harvest of works worth admiring. Some were as good or even possibly superior to the works of the previous years but their flaws and qualities were precisely the same that had been debated *ad nauseam*. A feeling of general discomfort and stagnation gradually developed, awaiting the advent of the man, the idea or the work that would be capable of reviving energies, enthusing a new spirit and stirring up art out of its dullness.

At that time precisely a whole chain of events occurred, the importance of which people of the time could not realise. They appear to us, however, as the portents of a new faith, the revelation of which was awaited. On several occasions, works containing elements of poetry focused on reality praised by Géricault were exhibited. Since *The Readers* in 1840, Meissonier had accustomed the public to meticulous accuracy. The opening of a Spanish gallery at the Louvre in 1848 showed the example of masters filled with an intense naturalist feeling. The daguerreotype was invented in 1839 and photography focused everybody's attention on views of direct reality once again. At the same time, Balzac, Stendhal and George Sand analysed contemporary life.

Thus realism crept into art and society through obscure and complex mechanisms. At first it only seemed to be claiming a small place but soon it asserted itself as the only truth and that it was up to the realist to regenerate the arts. At the last Exhibitions of the Monarchie de Juillet, two young painters had a modest start as no-one, not even themselves, guessed their potential. Then came the 1848 Revolution and Courbet and Millet discovered their own genius in the middle of the universal turmoil. Amidst a blaze of publicity they proclaimed the beliefs that were at the core of artistic battles. Of course some artists whose soul was definitely Romantic were going to remain: neither Delacroix nor Berlioz or Préault would give up their ideals and they could neither be forgotten nor despised. They would remain a reference for young people and, in a way, would continue to have more influence than ever. However, the continuing action of Romanticism would be of a different kind now, somewhat pacified and somewhat historical. In 1848 a new period started for the arts; Romantic times were over.

Caspar David Friedrich,
On the Sailing Boat, 1818-1820.
Oil on canvas, 71 x 56 cm.
The State Hermitage Museum,
St Petersburg.

Charles-François Grenier de Lacroix,
called **Charles-François Lacroix de
Marseille**, *A Mediterranean Harbour
Scene at Sunset,* 18th century.
Oil on canvas, 45.8 x 61 cm.
Private collection.

Richard Parkes Bonington,
Boats by the Normandy Shore,
c. 1823-1824. Oil on canvas,
33.5 x 46 cm. The State Hermitage
Museum, St Petersburg.

III. The Romantic Inspiration

Was the movement that we have just described only a violent bout of fever? Was it anything more than exaggeration and distortion? Did it only have a superficial and, when all is said and done, perhaps regrettable influence on artists? Was it going to be remembered as a movement marked by a strong and rampant taste for trinkets, cheap rubbish and mundane anecdotes, a movement mostly interested in subjects taken from fiction or history and easy to turn into vivid scenes? Those subjects corresponded to the fashion of the time, and if Romanticism had been limited to illustrating books and popular historical stories it would then be difficult to understand why it faced such strong resistance. If it was only made of mannerism and failings would it have kept raising so much passion and would it have remained polemical a century later?

Romanticism actually marked a general change of minds. As mentioned at the beginning of this book, it had expressed itself in all areas of human thinking and in all activities; it had had a deep impact on the arts. The works that it had influenced were linked together not just by superficial analogy but were closely related. They had been created according to the same norms and had used similar methods. It is those norms and methods that we are now going to try to unveil.

A Romantic person was first of all sensitive and someone on whom logic and pure ideas had little impact. It was a knowledgeable person whose actions were based on intuition: as a statesman, he would obey a generous or imaginary impetus; as a writer or poet his thinking was taking shape in images. All the more so for artists, who had no interest in abstraction but were indeed visionary. Others tried to draw a perfect type, a pure ideal beauty out of the diversity of humankind, but the Romantic, on the contrary, saw vivid creatures, all different and all touching in some way. He would develop friendships with certain individuals but was never exclusive and, in fact, was ready to change as he feared monotony more than anything else. In turn he would be interested in hook-nosed, pug-nosed, turned up-nosed people, slim or stocky types. He was seduced by unexpected appearances: irregular faces, deformities, alterations caused by illnesses and age. He was accused of cherishing ugliness whilst looking for character above all. Nature provided him with an infinite diversity of individuals and he could not see Apollo anywhere. If, by a miracle, Apollo were to spring up in front of his eyes, he would not represent the god in a fixed eternal attitude but would show him changing all the time, always different from himself because of the miracle of life. The classical man ignored it or, at least, always tried to fight against it whilst the Romantic observed it with pleasure and saw the source of beauty in it. The lines and volumes that the classicist aspired to give balance to according to blind geometry were perceived by the

Caspar David Friedrich, *Dreamer (Ruins of the Oybin Monastery)*, c. 1835. Oil on canvas, 27 x 21 cm. The State Hermitage Museum, St Petersburg.

Romantics as a sacred interaction of internal forces. Flesh quivered, blood ran, muscles tensed. Man was a magnificent machine: his shapes were not abstract calligraphy but they expressed the workings of physiological life. Catching life in action and movement before it was finished, observing the short instants when, guided by passion and under the pressure of dramatic circumstances, life reached a paroxysm, avoiding what pretended to be constant and celebrating the transitory and short-lived in life: these were the joys of the artist.

In studios, models would wrap themselves in indifferent clothes with more or less harmonious folds. Man would dress according to the climate he lived in, his needs and his tastes; his dressing style would reflect his personality and participate in his restlessness and existence itself.

To finish, man was not an isolated creature in the middle of a silent world. Life was all around him. Animals ran, flew or crawled, being moved (like humans) by a subtle system of forces. There were tangible affinities between man and animals. Less complex by nature, they provided the eye with sights which man could not rival. Nature was not an empty architectural structure, mere décor or background. It was full of elementary beings, close to us, visible or invisible, and even the things in it were constantly changing. The landscapes that seemed most stable were continually changing with leaves trembling in the wind, birds singing, light changing. It was a source of endless and renewed wonder. Inhabited by all those lives, nature itself seemed alive. One might consider it a form of pantheism except that the Romantics did not care about philosophical concepts so much. They only knew that their feelings and thoughts expanded in forests, at the seaside, or in mountains: if they were tormented, their restlessness calmed down. They were thankful to nature for that soothing action. Unlike poets who revolted against it because it did not echo their love experiences, Romantic artists paid tribute to the maternal and consoling quality of nature.

Though their universal sympathy went out in many directions, Romantic artists were in fact looking for themselves and, through their prodigal love for so many things and beings, they actually cherished themselves. Their curiosity was eager because their souls had an inextinguishable need of feeding. They never watched anything with dispassionate eyes, simply for the pleasure of knowledge: they would never forget themselves. One did not expect scientific testimony from any of them. They liked truth and wanted to be sincere, but their subjectivity and lyricism could not help but distort reality.

If he happened to be a man of rare genius, endowed with a whole set of exceptional and superior qualities that enabled him to think, suffer and be thrilled more than other mediocre human beings, the Romantic artist put fervent passion into his work as well as a taste for dramatisation and, in the early years of Romanticism, a dark mood which would get lighter with time but without ever reaching actual joyfulness. Even if he was a powerful worker merely admired for his skills, like Decamps or Barye, the complexity of his expressive moods and sometimes the surfeit and subtlety of details would be enough to prove that he belonged to a tormented generation.

John Constable,
Salisbury Cathedral from The Bishop's Ground, 1823.
Oil on canvas, 87.6 x 111.8 cm.
Victoria & Albert Museum, London.

Ivan Aivazovsky,
The Ninth Wave, 1850.
Oil on canvas, 221 x 332 cm.
The State Russian Museum,
St Petersburg.

Before starting a painting, Delacroix gathered information carefully, but once he had started work he could not bear the presence of models who put him off. The repulsion that he felt for his time is a more surprising paradox. The Flemish and Venetian artists whose influence he claimed, Véronèse and Rubens, had magnified the human beings and things around them. Not only did they take pleasure in their art, they thrived on the spirit of beauty in which they lived. They cherished their times and surroundings, in which they found allegory, history and religion. But the Romantic man felt ill at ease in his century: life in his time was dull, monuments were ugly and clothes shapeless. The crowd was merely eager for vulgar pleasures. Artists were isolated because they were different and misunderstood by their contemporaries. An object of vain ridicule early in life, these deplorable sentiments solidified through the trials of sarcasm and persecution throughout an artist's career.

Thus the Romantic man felt like escaping for, by a unique coincidence, he was born in the most hostile terrain: anywhere else and in any other time his genius would have been encouraged. Yet the Romantic landscape painters had abandoned Italy to take their easels to France. There were two main reasons for this: firstly, Italy was too imbued with classicism, and secondly, for a long time the Romantics were only interested in aspects of their native land that had not been damaged by human action. They ran away from modern cities, villages, cultivated plains, agricultural sites. They were inspired by high mountains and storms at sea, and they took hold of Fontainebleau because it embodied the majesty of untouched nature only fifteen miles from Paris.

For the rest, they tried most things and one would struggle to find another period in which inspiration would have been looked for in so many diverse or possibly scattered ways.

Most Romantics did not have a strong religious faith, but neither were they followers of Voltaire and generally they observed some form of pious decorum. They were not remarkable theologians, which possibly limited their scope or power, but their wild sensitivity gave them a sense of the mysteries beyond us and encouraged them to express the human sides of sacred narratives in particular.

The craze for history that occurred in the nineteenth century had deep causes that cannot be analysed here. The shape that history took was, however, highly Romantic and it made its way into literature, theatre and public balls under that form. Having located in the past a *joie de vivre* quite lacking in the present, Romantic artists played a role in a quasi universal movement. It would not be wrong to say that they had been awaited. Before them, the troubadour style had brought period costumes, armour, castles and banners back into fashion. Those images had to be filled with spirit and that is what the Romantics did. It is easy to make fun of the Romantic bric-à-brac, rags and clothes nowadays, to laugh at their flaws, their choice of appearance, haircuts and beards that were meant to embody the genius of Venice or the Middle Ages. Would it be fair to judge the quality of fireworks based on what is left after they are over? Such abundance, that seems silly to us, was brand new then and all the more attractive since it followed the

John Constable,
*The Opening of Waterloo Bridge
(Whitehall Stairs, June 18th, 1817),* 1832.
Oil on canvas, 130.8 x 218 cm.
Tate Gallery, London.

John Robert Cozens,
Lake of Vico between Rome and
Florence, 1783.
Graphite and watercolour on paper.
Yale Center for British Art, New Haven.

John Constable,
Dedham Lock and Mill, c. 1818.
Oil on canvas, 70 x 91 cm.
Private collection.

emptiness of classical décor. There were undoubtedly flaws in it but not everything was wrong. Artists tried hard to gather documents: Delacroix's meticulous drawings in his notebooks give testimony to it. Besides, they were not archaeologists. The spark of colours and shapes pleasing to the eye was an attempt to try to communicate directly with human beings in whom they saw an immense energy that seemed to be lacking in their narrow-minded century. Delacroix's power of evocation is so obvious that there is no need to insist on it: far from being superfluous or parasitical, every detail in his paintings helps to create life. He was a true witness of the dramas that he represented: before our eyes, we can see the crusaders laying siege to Constantinople, people cutting each other's throats on the bridge of Taillebourg, fighting in the mud around Nancy. But what Delacroix accomplished had been prepared by others. France raised a lot of interest and English history appeared particularly inspirational.

However, even when they fought classicism most violently, when they thought themselves saturated with Greeks and Romans, the Romantics had not totally put aside Antiquity. Nevertheless, Antiquity was a model debated amongst others and not the untouchable absolute and definite truth that it had been in the past. It became an historical period like any other in the chain of human history. In front of the arch of victory that he had just gone through under burning sun and surrounded by the sound of fanfares, Trajan was going forth on a nervous horse, and the woman who disturbed the procession by throwing her dead child at his feet caused disorder in which trumpets, standards and costumes moved about restlessly in a golden dusty haze.

Does the imagination of artists seem more rebellious because they took imaginary heroes from novelists or poets rather than from reading history books? The colours that Ariosto, Dante, Shakespeare, Byron, Walter Scott or Goethe had given to their characters were more pronounced, and life was the only thing that really mattered for the Romantics. Hamlet, Don Juan, Orlando Furioso were as vivid and fleshy as Saint Louis or Gaston de Foix. From an artistic point of view, there was no difference between the two types of character. As for what the Romantics chose to read, it was neither a matter of chance nor of personal fancy but rather the consequences of general circumstances. They read what was read around them and saw the shows that were on at the time. They were attracted by the works that enthused contemporary writers because they breathed in the same atmosphere.

However, there is one immense field unrelated to history that literature opened up and that Romantic artists took up and liked tremendously. After Dante and Goethe they trod on the paths of the fantastic and the beyond. Goethe guided Delacroix and Berlioz towards the witches' sabbath; Ary Scheffer represented the ballad of Lenore and Raffet the Nocturnal Review. There is no need to say that in the realms of the possible and the impossible the same instinct for concrete details was displayed. Barye modelled the hippogriff that took Angelica and Roger away with the most meticulous physiological verisimilitude.

There was no need for historians and poets to escape the dullness of the time; the past was still present and it surrounded and besieged one if one looked at the

monuments that it had left behind. *Notre-Dame de Paris* by Victor Hugo sums up the fervour with which old stones were revived and were avenged for centuries of oblivion. However, long before that epic resurrection, painters, drawers and architects went to collect the marvels scattered throughout Europe. A large survey was opened by the *Voyages pittoresques et romantiques dans l'ancienne France*, directed by Baron Taylor and Bonington as well as Isabey gave invaluable contributions towards it, which were widely talked of.

Escapism in time but also in space. After Poussin and Claude Lorrain, Roman landscape appeared like an empty décor. For artists Italy was nothing more than a wonderful museum. Before Delacroix, Bonington praised the splendour of Venice, the charm, the strange flavours, the unique physiognomy which had not been spotted by previous centuries. The poetry of the lagoon, of the palaces with their stone filigree, of the silent water and of the shape of gondolas appealed to eyes and hearts that were able to be moved by it. The moon over the Grand Canal was an invitation to a long reverie, which was new; the rooms of the Palace of the Doges, magnified by Tintoretto and Veronese, awaited the coming of Marin Faliero, of the Foscaris or of the moor Othello who had just got married to the daughter of senator Brabantio. The Greek War of Independence drew further attention to the East which, since the expedition to Egypt, had not been forgotten. Imagination was fired by incomplete and second-hand information. Without leaving their studios, artists praised the heroism of the Greeks. They built up a luxurious Orient ornamented with all the wealth that they could not access and sparkling with all the gems of the *Arabian Nights*. Odalisques replaced recumbent Venuses. But soon some looked for better information. The capture of Algiers started a new period; the East seemed closer and more accessible.

To finish, there was one other source of inspiration, which is hardly surprising considering the anxiety of those men used to looking for stimulation and who turned to historians and poets to try to access life. They spent a lot of time in museums, not just to look for advice and technical examples but also to fire their imaginations by contact with generous masters. They would have liked to live in the radiance of the Titian, Michelangelo and Rubens and they sometimes believed that they were transported near to them.

Thus the Romantic artist plunged into the past, looked for exotic landscapes and inspiration from the great masters in order to feed his sensitivity. Eager for authenticity, he always needed artificial stimulation. He wanted to express everything and was unable to forget himself so, whatever the topic, it was always coloured by his personality. The Romantics were not interested in immediate sights or daily reality; simplicity and calmness did not move them. They ran after what was under tension, exceptional, excessive and full of character. As they moved out of a period of narrow certainty when they were left to their own devices with no other guidance than their instinct, they were painfully initiated into freedom and were admirable for their élan, their desire to embrace everything and for the wild dreams of their unappeased hearts.

Joseph Mallord William Turner,
Ulysses Deriding Polyphemus –
Homer's Odyssey, 1829.
Oil on canvas, 132.5 x 203 cm.
The National Gallery, London.

IV. The Expressive Moods of Romanticism

he imagination of Romantic artists was full of colourful visions and resonant or visual harmonies. How did they find the suitable concrete means to express them? How did they carry out their work? Painters, sculptors and musicians all had their own language and specific techniques. However, they developed them from a common mould. It is interesting to try to define the artists' intentions as they were entering their studios. The Romantic artist claimed the same freedom in the practical making of a work as in the concepts behind it. He would not follow any conventional rule such as the conception of a type of beauty, the predominance of drawing or melody over colour and orchestration, systems of composition, balance, symmetry or purity. The knowledge and understanding of great masters and of the great artistic movements shows how vain those concepts can be. In the past, students who knew only the work of their patron might believe that he alone held the truth. But from then on, the treasures of the past were unveiled and accessible, and one had to admit that geniuses expressed themselves using the most diverse and sometimes opposite methods. It was absurd to choose between them as they were all worth admiring. Widened understanding opens up our eyes and allows freedom to break in; museums and libraries were a source of liberation.

It was also prejudice that was behind the made-up hierarchy that had been built up between the different arts and genres. Historical painters thought themselves superior because they dealt with mythology and memories from Greece and Rome. They looked down on genre painting and, besides, did not see any difference between painters who represented domestic scenes or décor and those who praised the Revolution or Napoleon. It was preposterous that certain sizes were reserved for certain subjects. The love affair between Mars and Venus was allowed colossal dimensions whilst the *Raft of the Medusa* was reduced to the size of a painting standing on an easel!

The limitation imposed on the various art forms as well as the barriers put up between them were also mostly arbitrary. It was wrong to assert that sculpture dealt only with plastics, that painting only expressed shapes and music only sounds. Every art form had the capacity to reflect the universe. Of course it would not do it by speaking to our reason as literature might, but, beyond reason, beyond what could be expressed with words, it could reach and move the deepest core of our being. The expressive power of the artist was only limited by his genius. Besides, at a time when literature created music with the rhythm of style and painting with the images it suggested, why should painting be a deaf form of art and music a blind? The Romantic artist was interested in transposing techniques from one art form to another. With his

Ary Scheffer,
St Augustine and his Mother St Monica,
1855.
Oil on canvas, 146.5 x 114.3 cm.
Musée du Louvre, Paris.

Symphonie en blanc majeur, Théophile Gautier competed both with painting and music. The Romantic landscape painters gave impressions of freshness and silence and Berlioz depicted a capital execution and a witches' sabbath in his *Symphony fantastique*.

Thus the artist was capable of delivering the total gamut of sensations and feelings. He could express himself fully. Through the process of carrying out the work, inspiration was enriched by the shapes it was taking in order to be expressed. However ardent and fruitful the creative spark might have been, the technical production of the work revealed beauty that seemed to stem from the material itself. The initial theme grew thicker and more luxurious; it became enriched with variations and harmonics. In trying to communicate something to others the artist discovered himself. All his work was influenced by his personality and to try to limit or dissimulate it would diminish its quality of the work. External finish and impersonal perfection seemed dull. One is constantly reminded of the presence of the author in the work through the mark of a brushstroke, a fingerprint, some uncontrolled stroke or a modification.

Such a frame of mind forced artists to work out their technique by themselves. They could not get from anyone else a ready-made tool that would be suited to their own thoughts. They were not so arrogant that they thought that they could learn everything by themselves however. They looked for education and were not self-taught. They asked for lessons from the École des beaux-arts. After *Dante and Virgil*, Delacroix returned to Guérin's studio, carried out some academic work and took part in competitions; Berlioz made continuous efforts to win the Prix de Rome. But they did not accept ready-made recipes and developed their technical skills in museums and libraries, through meditation and personal experimentation. They were accused of ignorance because their methods were disconcerting and different from previous habits. Most of them, however, were impatient to show their work; they made their début still young and with more boldness than skill. Yet in feverish and enthusiastic times, quick intuitions made up for methodical studies. Besides, the noise made around their works did not go to their heads for they wanted to perfect themselves. They often worried about technical issues; they looked for original combinations and experimented with new recipes, which was sometimes detrimental to the long term success of their works. Chemistry provided them with new colours such as cadmium, and the symphony orchestra was enriched by a whole series of new wind instruments. Technical anxiety naturally accompanied the anxiety of their thinking. The Romantics tried to diversify their moods of expression. Lithography, etching, and materials such as wood attracted them.

Is it possible to draw out Romantic practices that were common to all art forms? They never felt obliged to respect reality absolutely. They claimed the right to emphasise character, accentuate expressions and work on shapes. They did it discreetly or excessively, well or badly, moulding humanity again and again, as in the case of Delacroix, or systematically distorting things and people as Préault or David d'Angers did.

They could not stand bareness and plainness. They avoided clarity, straight lines and sharp edges. The basic tendencies of Romanticism consisted of thickening canvas,

developing orchestration, increasing accents and accidents, developing décor and becoming complicated with no fear of density or confusion. Romantic artists wanted to get rid of passivity or subordinate it to their power, swap geometry for dynamism, give up the precision that satisfies only the mind and, instead, resort to the senses and the soul. In everything they preferred life over order and obeyed passion. Classicism brought painting closer to sculpture and sculpture closer to architecture, the splendour of which was based on stability and permanence. But the efforts of the Romantic artist went totally in the opposite direction. He liked the short-lived, knocked about architecture, made sculpture picturesque, painting musical, literature picturesque and musical. Music reflected Romanticism more than any other art form because it was the most flowing, the most immaterial, penetrating and unspecified.

Romanticism could not be a single accident that occurred briefly and unexpectedly in the artistic evolution of the nineteenth century, with no origins and no consequences. It reflected one of the essential aspects of human genius: sensitivity versus rationality. There has not been a period without a Romantic element to it. Nowadays, to talk of the Romanticism of the classics has become commonplace. It would be just as relevant to analyse the classicism of the Romantics. It would be absurd to imagine artists totally devoid of logic or feeling. Because of influences between which one could see some analogies, certain periods were more favourable to Romantic expansion, for example the Hellenistic period or flamboyant Gothic. The seventeenth and eighteenth centuries were marked by the fieriness, exaggeration and Romanticism of the Baroque; Romanticism in the nineteenth century was in many ways a return to the Baroque tradition, a form of renewal or extension of it

So why was Romanticism thought so scandalous? As previously discussed, it faced a school of recent origins and which had plenty of credit, a school whose tendencies were in tune with the national spirit. The taste for balance, clarity and reason of the latter was hostile to Romanticism. Only a minority of artists, who were ardent and magnificent but limited in numbers, was fascinated by it. They would have been supported or at least well received if they had used more familiar methods to express themselves. But the usual language was not suitable. New forms surprised people and disoriented them. Most of those people did not resist Romanticism because they supported a different side but because they genuinely could not understand it. Thus the Romantic battle sometimes took the appearance of a technical quarrel but in reality there was a close link between technique and inspiration.

Carl Spitzweg,
The Writer, 19th century.
Oil on canvas. Kunsthaus, Munich.

Richard Parkes Bonington,
A Scene on the French Coast, c. 1825.
Watercolour and pencil on paper,
21.3 x 34.2 cm. Tate Gallery, London.

Conclusion

*I*n the eternal battle between feeling and rationality, Romanticism gave priority to sensitivity over logic, to images over pure ideas. Other periods that we have mentioned have known similar movements. Undoubtedly there will be comparable returns in the future.

Romanticism was preceded by a long period of preparation: it was not borne out of the crisis that made its development easy. It had long been waiting for the time when it could blossom. Similarly, it did not disappear in one day when the atmosphere changed. It gave way but did not die out when other tendencies took power. It continued to have a direct impact and a general influence on art in general. Its echo can still be heard by us today.

The protagonists, those who had started to produce works under the Romantic banner, kept working. Age and atmosphere impacted on them but did not change them drastically. Romanticism kept recruiting disciples after 1848. Most of all, it gradually overcame the resistance of the public. Romantic artists have now gained the popularity that they failed to obtain at the time of their battles. The Exhibition of 1855 was their first apotheosis. Since then, official recognition has kept on growing and their main works have entered museums. They have played a role in sharpening our sensitivity, in making it more flexible – and still do.

Besides, Romanticism has had a general influence. It has proclaimed freedom in the realm of the arts. In claiming for everyone the absolute right to express himself according to his own personality, it first fought for its own beliefs. At the same time and in a brotherly way it has encouraged the development of all tendencies, those with which it felt sympathetic and also those which fought against it and worked at destroying it. Thus a desire for tolerance grew and, in the end, appeared normal to everyone. Still nowadays many artists think nothing of values that can be created outside certain rules but even the hard core defenders of rules and discipline would not dare to ostracise anyone.

Mutual respect has become a doctrine. Nowadays no-one would venture to formulate criteria for what is beautiful. Romanticism managed to convince us of the relative quality of beauty. Thanks to it we recognise for each country, each period, each artist the right to choose its ideal and its norms. This is salutary: it allows us to watch with shrewd eyes, reconcile the dead and do justice to them. It encourages the birth of genius in the present and future. It also allows us to enjoy more things. We are not resistant to claims and open a friendly heart to new revelations.

A last word. Romanticism brought together art and life in a close embrace. It injected an aesthetic dimension into everything. The development and importance of

Théodore Chassériau,
The Artist's Sisters, 1843.
Oil on canvas, 180 x 135 cm.
Musée du Louvre, Paris.

art criticism and art history give testimony to it. Since then it has become commonplace that writers express their artistic feelings and impressions publicly. Our life has been enriched and ennobled. For all those reasons we should be thankful to this small group of feverish and generous young people who, a century ago and at a time when a materialistic civilisation was a threat to spirituality, came with the impudent but also invincible force of their youth to praise spiritual values and claim the supremacy of the Ideal.

Ary Scheffer,
Margaret at the Fountain, 1858.
Oil on canvas, 160 x 101 cm.
The Wallace Collection, London.

Théodore Géricault,
The Madwoman or *The Obsession of Envy,* c. 1819-1820.
Oil on canvas, 72 x 58 cm.
Musée des Beaux-Arts, Lyon.

William Blake,
Plate from Europe: A Prophecy, 1794.
Etching and watercolour, 37.5 x 27 cm.
Glasgow University Library, Glasgow.

A PROPHECY

The deep of winter came;
    What time the secret child,
Descended thro' the orient gates of the eternal day:
War ceas'd, & all the troops like shadows fled
    to their abodes.

Then Enitharmon saw her sons & daughters rise around.
Like pearly clouds they meet together in the crystal house:
And Los, possessor of the moon, joy'd in the peaceful night:
Thus speaking while his num'rous sons shook their bright fiery wings

    Again the night is come
That strong Urthona takes his rest,
And Urizen unloos'd from chains
Glows like a meteor in the distant north
Stretch forth your hands and strike the elemental strings!
Awake the thunders of the deep,

Extracts from Literary Texts

Jean-Jacques Rousseau
(1712-1778)

Reveries of the Solitary Walker

First walk

So now I am alone in the world, with no brother, neighbour or friend, nor any company left me but my own. The most sociable and loving of men has with one accord been cast out by all the rest. With all the ingenuity of hate they have sought out the cruellest torture for my sensitive soul, and have violently broken all the threads that bound me to them. I would have loved my fellow-men in spite of themselves. It was only by ceasing to be human that they could forfeit my affection. So now they are strangers and foreigners to me; they no longer exist for me, since such is their will. But I, detached as I am from them and from the whole world, what am I? This must now be the object of my inquiry. Unfortunately, before setting out on this quest, I must glance rapidly at my present situation, for this is a necessary stage on the road that leads from them to myself.

After the fifteen years or more that this strange state of affairs has lasted, I still imagine that I am suffering from indigestion and dreaming a bad dream, from which I shall wake with my pain gone to find myself once again in the midst of my friends. Yes, I must surely have slipped unwillingly from waking into sleep, or rather from life into death. Wrenched somehow out of the natural order, I have plunged into an incomprehensible chaos where I can make nothing out, and the more I think about my present situation, the less I can understand what had become of me.

How indeed could I ever have foreseen the fate that lay in wait for me? How can I envisage it even today, when I have succumbed to it? Could I, in my right mind, suppose that I, the very same man who I was then and am still today, would be taken beyond all doubt for a monster, a poisoner, an assassin, that I would become the horror of the human race, the laughing-stock of the rabble, that all the recognition I would receive from passers-by would be to be spat upon, and that an entire generation would of one accord take pleasure in burying me alive? At the time of this amazing transformation, my instinctive reaction was one of consternation. My emotion and indignation plunged me into a fever which has taken all of ten years to abate, and during this time, as I lurched from fault to fault, error to error, and folly to folly, my imprudent behaviour provided those who control my fate with weapons which they have most skilfully used to settle my destiny irrevocably.

Caspar David Friedrich, *The Wanderer above the Mists*, c. 1817-1818.
Oil on canvas, 94.8 x 74.8 cm. Hamburger Kunsthalle, Hamburg.

James MacPherson
(1736–1796)

Fragments of Ancient Poetry

ARGUMENT.

Lathmon, a British prince, taking advantage of Fingal's absence on expedition in Ireland made a descent on Morven, and advanced within sight of Selma, the royal residence. Fingal arrived in the mean time, and Lathmon retreated to a hill, where his army was surprised by night, and himself taken prisoner by Ossian and Gaul the son of Morni. [some printings include: "This exploit of Gaul and Ossian bears a near resemblance to the beautiful episode of Nisus and Euryalus in Virgil's ninth Aeneid."] The poem opens, with the first appearance of Fingal on the coasts of Morven, and ends, it may be supposed, about noon of the next day.

LATHMON: A POEM.

SELMA, thy halls are silent. There is no sound in the woods of Morven. The wave tumbles alone on the coast. The silent beam of the sun is on the field. The daughters of Morven come forth, like the bow of the shower; they look towards green Erin for the white sails of the king. He had promised to return, but the winds of the north arose!

Who pours from the eastern hill, like a stream of darkness? It is the host of Lathmon. He has heard of the absence of Fingal. He trusts in the wind of the north. His soul brightens with joy. Why dost thou come, O Lathmon? The mighty are not in Selma. Why comest thou with thy forward spear? Will the daughters of Morven fight? But stop, O mighty stream, in thy course! Does not Lathmon behold these sails? Why dost thou vanish, Lathmon, like the mist of the lake? But the squally storm is behind thee; Fingal pursues thy steps!

The king of Morven started from sleep, as we rolled on the dark-blue wave. He stretched his hand to his spear, and his heroes rose around. We knew that he had seen his fathers, for they often descended to his dreams, when the sword of the foe rose over the land; and the battle darkened before us. Whither hast thou fled, O wind? said the king of Morven. Dost thou rustle in the chambers of the south, and pursue the shower in other lands? Why dost thou not come to my sails, to the blue face of my seas? The foe is in the land of Morven, and the king is absent. But let each bind on his mail, and each assume his shield. Stretch every spear over the wave; let every sword be unsheathed. Lathmon is before us with his host: he that fled from Fingal on the plains of Lona. But he returns, like a collected stream, and his roar is between our hills.

Such were the words of Fingal. We rushed into Carmona's bay. Ossian ascended the hill; and thrice struck his bossy shield. The rock of Morven replied; and the bounding roes came forth. The foes were troubled in my presence: and collected their darkened host; for I stood, like a cloud on the hill, rejoicing in the arms of my youth.

John Constable, *Salisbury Cathedral from the Meadows*, 1831.
Oil on canvas, 151.8 x 189.9 cm. The National Gallery, London.

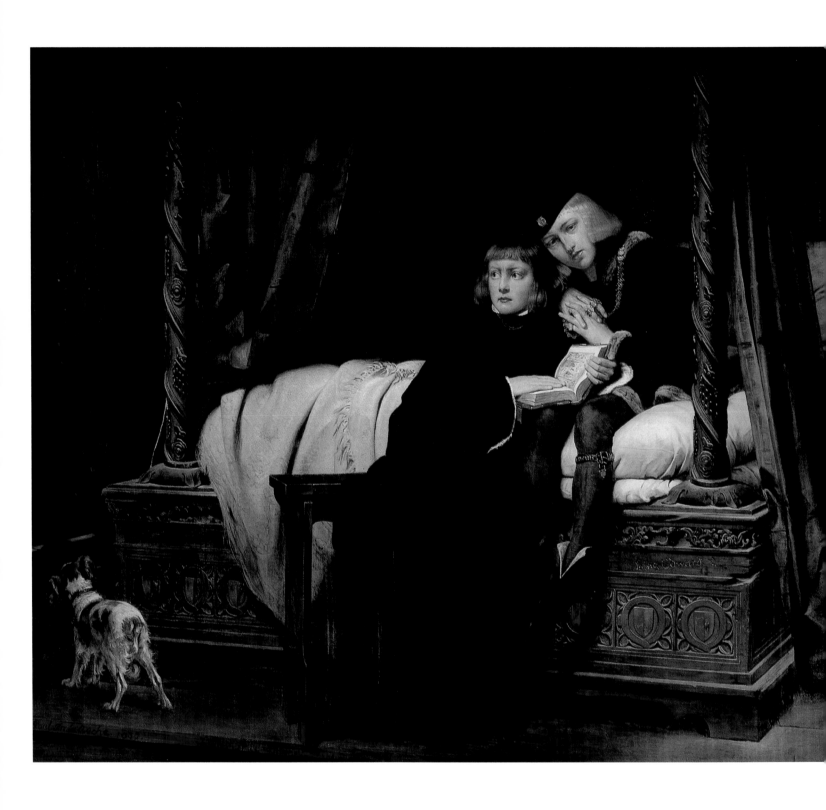

Hippolyte de La Roche, called **Paul Delaroche**, *Edward V (1470-1483) and Richard,*
Duke of York in the Tower (Les Enfants d'Édouard), 1831.
Oil on canvas, 181 x 215 cm. Musée du Louvre, Paris.

Johann Wolfgang von Goethe
(1749-1832)

Faust

NIGHT

(*A lofty-arched, narrow, Gothic chamber.*
FAUST,
in a chair at his desk, restless.)

FAUST

I've studied now Philosophy
And Jurisprudence, Medicine, –
And even, alas! Theology, –
From end to end, with labour keen;
And here, poor fool! with all my lore
I stand, no wiser than before:
I'm Magister – yea, Doctor – hight,
And straight or cross-wise, wrong or right,
These ten years long, with many woes,
I've led my scholars by the nose, –
And see, that nothing can be known!
That knowledge cuts me to the bone.
I'm cleverer, true, than those fops of teachers,
Doctors and Magisters, Scribes and Preachers;
Neither scruples nor doubts come now to smite me,
Nor Hell nor Devil can longer affright me.

For this, all pleasure am I foregoing;
I do not pretend to aught worth knowing,
I do not pretend I could be a teacher
To help or convert a fellow-creature.
Then, too, I've neither lands nor gold,
Nor the world's least pomp or honour hold –
No dog would endure such a curst existence!
Wherefore, from Magic I seek assistance,
That many a secret perchance I reach
Through spirit-power and spirit-speech,
And thus the bitter task forego
Of saying the things I do not know, –
That I may detect the inmost force
Which binds the world, and guides its course;
Its germs, productive powers explore,
And rummage in empty words no more!

O full and splendid Moon, whom I
Have, from this desk, seen climb the sky
So many a midnight,—would thy glow
For the last time beheld my woe!
Ever thine eye, most mournful friend,
O'er books and papers saw me bend;
But would that I, on mountains grand,
Amid thy blessed light could stand,
With spirits through mountain-caverns hover,
Float in thy twilight the meadows over,
And, freed from the fumes of lore that swathe me,
To health in thy dewy fountains bathe me!

William Blake
(1757-1827)

Poems

The Echoing Green

The sun does arise,
And make happy the skies;
The merry bells ring
To welcome the Spring;
The skylark and thrush,
The birds of the bush,
Sing louder around
To the bells' cheerful sound;
While our sports shall be seen
On the echoing Green.

Old John, with white hair,
Does laugh away care,
Sitting under the oak,
Among the old folk.
They laugh at our play,

And soon they all say,
"Such, such were the joys
When we all – girls and boys –
In our youth-time were seen
On the echoing Green."

Till the little ones, weary,
No more can be merry:
The sun does descend,
And our sports have an end.
Round the laps of their mothers
Many sisters and brothers,
Like birds in their nest,
Are ready for rest,
And sport no more seen
On the darkening green.

William Blake, Plate from *Europe: A Prophecy*, 1794.
Lithography, 23.3 x 16.8 cm. The British Museum, London.

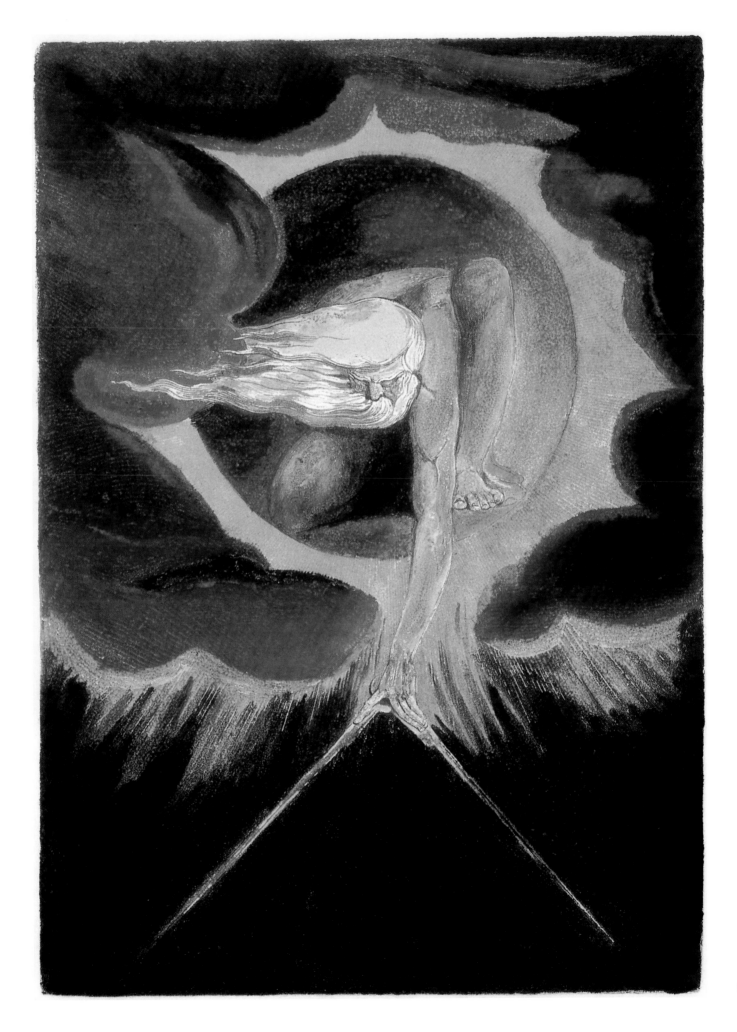

Johann Christoph Friedrich von Schiller
(1759–1805)

The Bride of Messina

Scene 1

A spacious hall, supported on columns, with entrances on both sides; at the back of the stage a large folding-door leading to a chapel.

DONNA ISABELLA in mourning;
the ELDERS OF MESSINA.

ISABELLA.

Forth from my silent chamber's deep recesses,
Grey Fathers of the State, unwillingly
I come; and, shrinking from your gaze, uplift
The veil that shades my widowed brows: the light
And glory of my days is fled forever!
And best in solitude and kindred gloom
To hide these sable weeds, this grief-worn frame,
Beseems the mourner's heart. A mighty voice
Inexorable – duty's stern command,
Calls me to light again.
Not twice the moon
Has filled her orb since to the tomb ye bore
My princely spouse, your city's lord, whose arm
Against a world of envious foes around
Hurled fierce defiance! Still his spirit lives
In his heroic sons, their country's pride:

Ye marked how sweetly from their childhood's bloom
They grew in joyous promise to the years
Of manhood's strength; yet in their secret hearts,
From some mysterious root accursed, upsprung
Unmitigable, deadly hate, that spurned
All kindred ties, all youthful, fond affections,
Still ripening with their thoughtful age; not mine
The sweet accord of family bliss; though each
Awoke a mother's rapture; each alike
Smiled at my nourishing breast! for me alone
Yet lives one mutual thought, of children's love;
In these tempestuous souls discovered else
By mortal strife and thirst of fierce revenge.

While yet their father reigned, his stern control
Tamed their hot spirits, and with iron yoke
To awful justice bowed their stubborn will:
Obedient to his voice, to outward seeming
They calmed their wrathful mood, nor in array
Ere met, of hostile arms; yet unappeased
Sat brooding malice in their bosoms' depths;
They little reek of hidden springs whose power
Can quell the torrent's fury:

Eugène Delacroix, *Greece on the Ruins of Messolonghi,* 1826.
Oil on canvas, 213 x 142 cm. Musée des Beaux-Arts, Bordeaux.

Lorenzo Bartolini, *Faith in God,* 1835.
Marble, h. : 93 cm. Museo Poldi Pezzoli, Milan.

Pietro Tenerani, *Psyche Abandoned,* 1818.
Marble, h. : 118 cm. Galleria d'arte moderna, Florence.

Germaine Necker, Baroness de Staël-Holstein, called Madame de Staël
(1766-1817)

Germany

Part II, Chapter XI

The word *Romantic* has been lately introduced in Germany to designate that kind of poetry which is derived from the songs of the troubadours; that which owes its birth to the union of chivalry and Christianity. If we do not admit that the empire of literature had been divided between paganism and Christianity, the North and the South, Antiquity and the Middle Ages, chivalry and the institutions of Greece and Rome, we shall never succeed in forming a philosophical judgement of ancient and modern taste.

We sometimes consider the word *classic* as synonymous with perfection. I use it at present with a different meaning, considering classic poetry as that of the ancients and Romantic poetry as that which is somehow connected with the traditions of chivalry. This division is equally suitable to the two eras of the world, that which preceded and that which followed the establishment of Christianity.

[…] The literature of the ancients is, among the moderns, a transplanted literature. Chivalrous literature or romance is indigenous and flourishes under the influence of our religion and our institutions. Writers, who imitate the ancients, have subjected themselves to the rules of strict taste alone; for, not being able to consult either their own nature or their own memories, it was necessary for them to conform to those laws by which the masterpieces of the ancients may be adapted to our taste; though the circumstances both political and religious, which gave birth to these masterpieces, are all entirely changed. But the poetry written in imitation of the ancients, however perfect in its kind, is seldom popular because in our days it has no connection with our national feelings.

[…] Our French poets are admired wherever there are cultivated minds, either in our own nation or in the rest of Europe; but they are quite unknown to the common people and even to the class of citizens in our towns because the arts, in France, are not, as elsewhere, natives of the very country in which their beauties are displayed.

[…] Romantic literature is alone capable of further improvement because, being rooted in our own soil, that alone can continue to grow and acquire fresh life: it expresses our religion, it recalls our history; its origin is ancient although not of classical Antiquity.

Classic poetry, before it comes home to us, must pass through our recollections of paganism: that of the Germans is the Christian era of the fine arts: it uses our personal impressions to excite strong and vivid emotions: the genius by which it is inspired speaks to our hearts immediately and seems to call forth the spirit of our own lives, of all phantoms at once the most powerful and the most terrible.

Francesco Hayez, *Portrait of Carlotta Chabert (Venus Playing with Two Doves),* 1830.
Oil on canvas, 183 x 137 cm. Cassa di Risparmio di Trento e Rovereto, Trento.

Benjamin Constant
(1767-1830)

Adolphe

First Chapter

My feeling of constraint with him had a great influence on my character. I was as timid as he but, being younger, I was more excitable and kept to myself all that I felt, made all my plans on my own and relied on myself to put them into effect. I considered the opinions, interest, assistance and even the mere presence of others as a hindrance and an obstacle. I developed the habit of never speaking of what I was doing, of enduring conversation only as a tiresome necessity and enlivening it by perpetual joking which made it less wearisome to me, and helped to hide any real thoughts. Hence a certain reserve with which my friends reproach me even today and a difficulty in conversing seriously which I still find hard to overcome. From the same cause sprang an ardent desire for independence, a considerable impatience with all ties and an invincible terror at forming new ones. I felt at ease only when quite alone and such, even now, is the effect of that disposition that in the most trifling circumstances when I have to choose between two courses of action, a human face disturbs me and my natural impulse is to flee in order to deliberate in peace. However, I did not possess the depths of egoism which such a character would seem to indicate. Though only interested in myself I was but faintly interested. Unconsciously I bore in my heart a need for sympathy which, not being satisfied, caused me to abandon one after another every object of my curiosity. This indifference to everything was further strengthened by the idea of death, an idea which had impressed itself upon me when I was very young. I have never been able to understand how men could so readily cease to be fully active upon this notion.

Henry Raeburn, *Reverend Robert Walker Skating on Duddingston Loch,* 1795.
Oil on canvas, 76.2 x 63.5 cm. National Gallery of Scotland, Edinburgh.

François René Chateaubriand, vicomte de Chateaubriand
(1768-1848)

René

In daytime I would lose my way on heath ended by forests. Any small thing would make me daydream: some dry leaf swept away by the wind, a little hut releasing smoke over the bare tops of the trees, a moth trembling in the north wind on the trunk of an oak, some isolated rock, a deserted pond where some withered rush would murmur! My eyes have often been attracted by the solitary steeple sticking out far away in the valley; often my eyes have followed birds of passage flying over my head. I imagined the unknown shores and distant climates where they were heading to. I wished that I had been on their wings. A secret instinct tormented me; I felt that I was myself but a traveller, but a voice from heaven seemed to be saying to me: 'Man, the season of your migration has not come yet; wait until the wind of death rises; then you will regret the flight towards those unknown regions that your heart is craving for.'

Rise up, desired storms that are meant to take away René to the lands of another life!

Saying that, I would walk hastily with a blazing face and the wind whistling in my hair. I could feel neither rain nor wintry weather and was tormented as if possessed by the demon of my heart.

Thomas Cole, *The Departure,* 1837.
Oil on canvas, 101 x 160 cm. Corcoran Gallery of Art, Washington, D.C.

Caspar David Friedrich, *The Polar Sea,* 1824.
Oil on canvas, 96.7 x 126.9 cm. Hamburger Kunsthalle, Hamburg.

William Wordsworth

(1770–1850)

Lyrical Ballads

The Thorn

I.

There is a thorn; it looks so old,
In truth you'd find it hard to say,
How it could ever have been young,
It looks so old and grey.
Not higher than a two-years' child,
It stands erect this aged thorn;
No leaves it has, no thorny points;
It is a mass of knotted joints,
A wretched thing forlorn.
It stands erect, and like a stone
With lichens it is overgrown.

II.

Like rock or stone, it is o'ergrown
With lichens to the very top,
And hung with heavy tufts of moss,
A melancholy crop:
Up from the earth these mosses creep,
And this poor thorn they clasp it round
So close, you'd say that they were bent
With plain and manifest intent,
To drag it to the ground;
And all had joined in one endeavour
To bury this poor thorn for ever.

Georg Philipp Friedrich Freiherr von Hardenberg, called Novalis
(1772-1801)

Hymn to Night

What living being, gifted with feeling, bestows not his love on the all joyful light?

Loves it before all the wonders spread out before him through regions of space, light undulating, colour-filled, raying its mild omnipresence by day?

As life's inmost soul, it is breathed by the giant world of restless stars that swim in its blue ocean, by the sparkling stone, the peaceful plant, by the creatures' many-fashioned ever-moving life and, above all, by the glorious strangers with the thoughtful eyes, the swinging gait and the sounding lips.

As a queen it summons each power of terrestrial nature to numberless changes and alone doth its presence reveal the full splendour on earth.

Downwards wend I way to Night, holy, inexpressible, secret-filled,

Far away lies the world, sunk in deep vault; how dreary, forlorn her abode! Deep melancholy

stirs in the chords of the breast, far-off memories, wishes of youth, dreams of childhood, short-lived joys and vain hopes of the long endured life come in grey garments, like evening mists after sunset.

Far-off lies the world with its motley pleasures.

Elsewhere doth the Night pitch its airy encampment.

What if it never returned to its faithful children?

Caspar David Friedrich, *Monk by Sea,* c. 1809.
Oil on canvas, 110 x 171.5 cm. Nationalgalerie, Berlin.

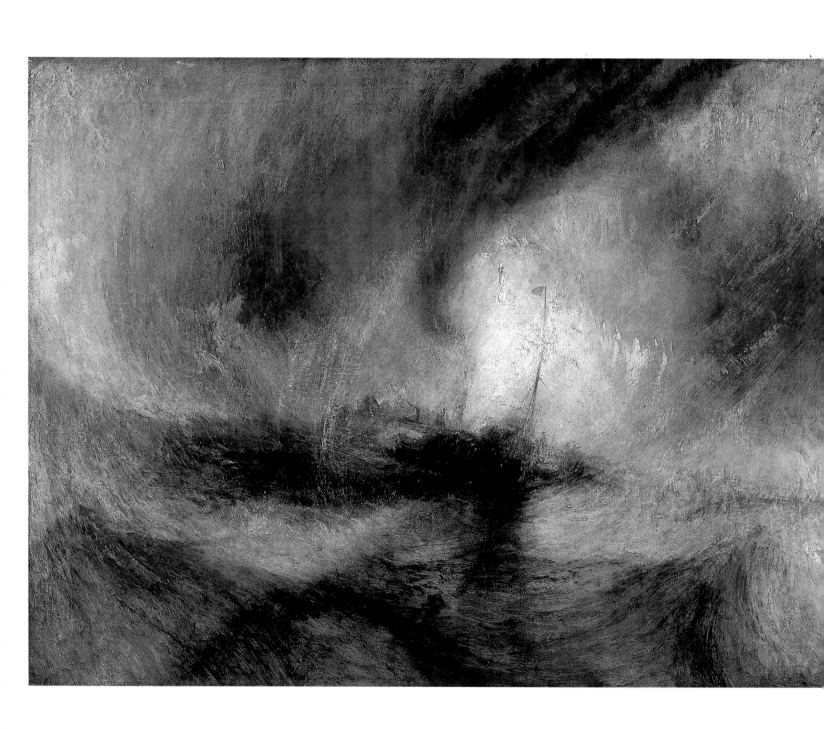

Joseph Mallord William Turner, *Snow Storm – Steam-Boat off a Harbour's Mouth,* 1842.
Oil on canvas, 91.4 x 121.9 cm. Tate Gallery, London.

What flows so cool, so refreshing, so full of hid tidings, to our hearts, and absorbs the soft air

of melancholy? Hast thou too a human heart, O dark night?

What holdest thou under thy mantle which steals unseen upon my soul, giving it strength?

A precious balm drops from thy hand, from the bundle of poppies. In sweet intoxication thou unfoldest the soul's heavy wings, and givest us dark, inexpressible joys: joyously frightened I see a dark, soft and meditative face bending over me and showing the cherished youth of the Mother under tangled locks. Light seems to me so empty and childish now – so joyful and blessed the day's farewell! – And it's only because the Night turns your followers away from you that you have sowed – in the immense space – luminous globes to proclaim your almighty power – your return – in the hours when you're away.

More heavenly than those flashing stars, in those wide spaces, seem to us the infinite eyes which the night in us opens. Farther see thou the palest of that numberless host. With no need for light, they look through the depths of a heart full of love, which fills with unspeakable joy a loftier space.

Praise to the Lord's queen! To the lofty proclaimer of holy worlds, to the nurturer of blissful love. Thou comest, tender beloved, the night is here. Now I am awake – for I am yours and mine – you've revealed to me that Night is life – you've made me man – Let the fire of the spirit consume my body so that, belonging no longer to earth, you and I are intimately mingled and the nuptial night last forever.

Friedrich von Schlegel
(1772-1829)

Philosophy of Life

LECTURE I

OF THE THINKING SOUL AS THE CENTRE OF CONSCIOUSNESS, AND OF THE FALSE PROCEDURE OF REASON.

"THERE are," says a poet as ingenious as profound, " more things in heaven and earth, than are dreamt of in our philosophy." This sentiment, which Genius accidentally let drop, is in the main applicable also to the philosophy of our own day; and, with a slight modification, I shall be ready to adopt it as my own. The only change that is requisite to make it available for my purpose would be the addition "and also between heaven and earth are there many things which are not dreamt of in our philosophy." And exactly because philosophy, for the most part, does nothing but dream – scientifically dream, it may be – therefore is it ignorant, ay, has no inkling even of much which, nevertheless, in all propriety it ought to know. It loses sight of its true object, it quits the firm ground where, standing secure, it might pursue its own avocations without let or hindrance, whenever, abandoning its own proper region, it either soars up to heaven to weave there its fine-spun webs of dialectics, and to build its metaphysical castles in the air, or else, losing itself on the earth, it violently interferes with external reality, and determines to shape the world according to its own fancy, and to reform it at will. Half-way between these two devious courses lies the true road; and the proper region of philosophy is even that spiritual inner life between heaven and earth.

Carl Gustav Carus, *Woman on a Stool,* 1824.
Oil on canvas, 42 x 33 cm. Gemäldegalerie, Dresden.

Ernst Theodor Amadeus Hoffmann
(1776-1822)

The Devil's Elixir

I stood up and wanted to go in the friar's; but I was terror-stricken in a strange way and, like in a bout of fever, it made my whole body shake. I preferred to go and see Prior Leonard. After having struggled to wake him up I told him what I had heard. The prior was frightened; he stood up hastily, asked me to go and get some consecrated candles and to go with him to friar Medardus's. I did as he had ordered and lit up the candles with the lamp in the corridor in front of the statue of the Lord's mother and we went up the stairs. Though we were all ears we did not hear the voice that had struck me before but, instead, there was a soft and agreeable ring of bells and we had the impression to be breathing in a delightful scent of roses.

We went nearer and the door opened: a tall strange man with a curly white beard and who was covered up with a purple coat came out. I was terror-stricken for I understood that it could only be a ghost as no stranger could force his way in the cloister but Leonard looked at him boldly in the eyes without uttering a single word.

Francisco de Goya y Lucientes, *Saturn Devouring One of his Children,* 1819-1823.
Plaster mounted on canvas, 146 x 83 cm. Museo Nacional del Prado, Madrid.

'The time is nearly up!' said the ghost with a muffled and solemn voice before disappearing in the dark corridor. My fear increased and I nearly dropped the candle that I was holding.

But the prior who, because of his faith and strong beliefs, does not like talking about spectres, took my arm and said to me: 'Let's go in Medardus's room.' We went in and found the friar – who had been very weak for a while – fighting for his life and unable to speak. We could only perceive a very weak death rattle. Leonard stayed by him whilst I went to ring the bell forcefully and wake the monks bawling: ' Get up! Get up! Friar Medardus is dying!'

They got up and none was missing when we went with candles and gathered around the dying friar. We were all plunged deep in grief and the sadness overcame my terror. We carried the friar into the church and laid him in front of the altar.

There, to our great surprise, he started to speak again and Leonard, after hearing the friar's confession, gave him absolution and Extreme Unction.

Immediately after we went in the chancel and started to sing funeral anthems for the salvation of the dying monk; but Leonard stayed close to him and talked with him. At the very moment when the bell rang twelve and a new day started, on 5th September 17.., Friar Medardus passed away in the arms of the prior.

Eugène Delacroix, *The Death of Sardanapalus*, 1827.
Oil on canvas, 392 x 496 cm. Musée du Louvre, Paris.

Thomas Couture, *Romans of the Decadence*, 1847.
Oil on canvas, 472 x 772 cm. Musée d'Orsay, Paris.

Joseph von Görres
(1776-1848)

Bayard, or the Death of the True Hero

As it was forced to beat a retreat from Milan, the French army commanded by Admiral Bonivet was chased heavily by the Spanish. Because the admiral had been wounded he let the knight Bayard take over. The latter charged at the enemy so vigorously for a couple of hours that it seemed possible that he could save the army. Indeed, both the artillery and the ensigns were safe when, at ten o'clock in the morning, a harquebus shot hit Bayard's flank and broke his spine. When he felt the hit he first shouted 'Jesus, O my Lord! I'm dead!' Then he kissed the crossing on his sword as a symbol of the Cross; he changed colour and as they saw him totter, his people came to take him out the mêlée. His friend d'Alègre tried to convince him but Bayard would not allow it. 'It's all over for me,' he said to them, 'I am dead and in the last moments I do not want to turn my back on the enemy for the first time in my life.' He had the strength to give the order to charge as he saw the Spanish beginning to progress. Then, with the help of a few Swiss soldiers, he was sat by a tree so that, as he said, he could face the enemy. His helper, who was a gentleman native from the Dauphiné and who was called Jacques Jeoffre, from Milieu, was in tears by him, as were his other servants. Bayard consoled them himself: ' It is God's will that I go to him; he kept me in this world long enough and I have been granted more good than I ever deserved.'

François Rude, *Napoleon Awakening to Immortality,* 1845.
Plaster, 215 x 195 x 96 cm. Musée d'Orsay, Paris.

Henri Beyle, called **Stendhal**

(1783-1842)

The Charterhouse of Parma

First Chapter

Milan in 1796

On 15th May 1796, General Bonaparte made his entry into Milan at the head of that young army which had shortly before crossed the bridge of Lodi and taught the world that after all these centuries Caesar and Alexander had a successor. The miracles of gallantry and genius of which Italy was a witness in the space of a few months aroused a slumbering people; only a week before the arrival of the French, the Milanese still regarded them as a mere rabble of brigands, accustomed invariably to flee before the troops of His Imperial and Royal Majesty; so much at least was reported to them three times weekly by a little news-sheet no bigger than one's hand, and printed on soiled paper.

In the Middle Ages the Republicans of Lombardy had given proof of a valour equal to that of the French, and deserved to see their city razed to the ground by the German Emperors. Since they had become *loyal subjects*, their great occupation was the printing of sonnets upon handkerchiefs of rose-coloured taffeta whenever the marriage occurred of a young lady belonging to some rich or noble family. Two or three years after that great event in her life, the young lady in question used to engage a devoted admirer: sometimes the name of *cicisbeo* chosen by the husband's family occupied an honourable place in the marriage contract. It was a far cry from these effeminate ways to the profound emotions aroused by the unexpected arrival of the French army. Presently there sprang up a new and passionate way of life. A whole people discovered, on 15th May 1796, that everything which until then it had respected was supremely ridiculous, if not actually hateful. The departure of the last Austrian regiment marked the collapse of the old ideas: to risk one's life became the fashion. People saw that, in order to be really happy after centuries of cloying sensations, it was necessary to love one's country with a real love and to seek out heroic actions. They had been plunged in the darkest night by the continuation of the jealous despotism of Charles V and Philip II; they overturned these monarchs' statues and immediately found themselves flooded with daylight.

John Martin, *The Great Day of His Wrath,* 1851-1853.
Oil on canvas, 196.5 x 303.2 cm. Tate Gallery, London.

Charles Lock Eastlake, *Lord Byron's 'Dream',* 1827.
Oil on canvas, 118.1 x 170.8 cm. Tate Gallery, London.

George Gordon, Lord Byron
(1788-1824)

The Prayer of Nature

Father of Light! great God of Heaven!
Hear'st thou the accents of despair?
Can guilt like man's be e'er forgiven?
Can vice atone for crimes by prayer?

Father of Light, on thee I call!
Thou see'st my soul is dark within;
Thou, who canst mark the sparrow's fall,
Avert from me the death of sin.

No shrine I seek, to sects unknown;
Oh, point to me the path of truth!
Thy dread Omnipotence I own;
Spare, yet amend, the faults of youth.

Let bigots rear a gloomy fane,
Let Superstition hail the pile,
Let priests, to spread their sable reign,
With tales of mystic rites beguile.

Shall man confine his Maker's sway
To Gothic domes of mouldering stone?
Thy temple is the face of day;
Earth, Ocean, Heaven thy boundless throne.

Shall man condemn his race to Hell,
Unless they bend in pompous form?
Tell us that all, for one who fell,
Must perish in the mingling storm?

Shall each pretend to reach the skies,
Yet doom his brother to expire,
Whose soul a different hope supplies,
Or doctrines less severe inspire?

Shall these, by creeds they can't expound,
Prepare a fancied bliss or woe?
Shall reptiles, grovelling on the ground,
Their great Creator's purpose know?

Shall those, who live for self alone,
Whose years float on in daily crime –
Shall they, by Faith, for guilt atone,
And live beyond the bounds of Time?

Father! no prophet's laws I seek, –
Thy laws in Nature's works appear; –
I own myself corrupt and weak,
Yet will I pray, for thou wilt hear!

Thou, who canst guide the wandering star,
Through trackless realms of aether's space;
Who calm'st the elemental war,
Whose hand from pole to pole I trace:

Thou, who in wisdom plac'd me here,
Who, when thou wilt, canst take me hence,
Ah! whilst I tread this earthly sphere,
Extend to me thy wide defence.

To Thee, my God, to thee I call!
Whatever weal or woe betide,
By thy command I rise or fall,
In thy protection I confide.

If, when this dust to dust's restor'd,
My soul shall float on airy wing,
How shall thy glorious Name ador'd
Inspire her feeble voice to sing!

But, if this fleeting spirit share
With clay the Grave's eternal bed,
While Life yet throbs I raise my prayer,
Though doom'd no more to quit the dead.

To Thee I breathe my humble strain,
Grateful for all thy mercies past,
And hope, my God, to thee again
This erring life may fly at last.

December 29, 1806.

Caspar David Friedrich, *Chalk Cliffs on Rügen,* 1818-1819.
Oil on canvas, 90 x 70 cm. Museum Oskar Reinhart am Stadtgarten, Winterthur.

Joseph Wright,
The Indian Widow, 1785.
Oil on canvas, 101.6 x 127 cm.
Derby Museum and Art Gallery, Derby.

Thomas Cole, *The Last of the Mohicans, Cora Kneeling at the Feet of Tamenund*, 1827.
Oil on canvas, 64.5 x 89 cm. Wadsworth Atheneum Museum of Art, Hartford.

James Fenimore Cooper
(1789-1851)

The Last of the Mohicans

Chapter I

"Mine ear is open, and my heart prepared: The worst is wordly loss thou canst unfold:
– Say, is my kingdom lost?"

Shakespeare

It was a feature peculiar to the colonial wars of North America, that the toils and dangers of the wilderness were to be encountered before the adverse hosts could meet. A wide and apparently an impervious boundary of forests severed the possessions of the hostile provinces of France and England. The hardy colonist, and the trained European who fought at his side, frequently expended months in struggling against the rapids of the streams, or in effecting the rugged passes of the mountains, in quest of an opportunity to exhibit their courage in a more martial conflict. But, emulating the patience and self-denial of the practised native warriors, they learned to overcome every difficulty; and it would seem that, in time, there was no recess of the woods so dark, nor any secret place so lovely, that it might claim exemption from the inroads of those who had pledged their blood to satiate their vengeance, or to uphold the cold and selfish policy of the distant monarchs of Europe.

Perhaps no district throughout the wide extent of the intermediate frontiers can furnish a livelier picture of the cruelty and fierceness of the savage warfare of those periods than the country which lies between the head waters of the Hudson and the adjacent lakes.

The facilities which nature had there offered to the march of the combatants were too obvious to be neglected. The lengthened sheet of the Champlain stretched from the frontiers of Canada, deep within the borders of the neighboring province of New York, forming a natural passage across half the distance that the French were compelled to master in order to strike their enemies. Near its southern termination, it received the contributions of another lake, whose waters were so limpid as to have been exclusively selected by the Jesuit missionaries to perform the typical purification of baptism, and to obtain for it the title of lake "du Saint Sacrement". The less zealous English thought they conferred a sufficient honor on its unsullied fountains, when they bestowed the name of their reigning prince, the second of the house of Hanover. The two united to rob the untutored possessors of its wooded scenery of their native right to perpetuate its original appellation of "Horican."

Alphonse de Lamartine
(1790-1869)

Poetical Meditations

The Lake

Thus always driven towards new shores,
Carried returnless away into eternal light,
On the Ocean of Ages will we never be able
To drop anchor one lone day?

O Lake! The year has hardly finished his career;
And near the cherished waves that she was to see
again,
Look! I come alone to sit down on this stone
Where you saw her sit down!

So you were roaring below on these profound rocks,
So you were breaking against their ragged sides;
So was the wind gently throwing foam from your
waves
Upon her adored feet.
One night, do you remember? We were rowing in
silence;
One only heard afar, over waves and under skies,
The sound of rowers who were striking in cadence
Your harmonious waves.

All of a sudden, some sounds unknown on earth
Struck the enchanted bank and bounced their echoes
back;
The wave was attentive, and the voice, dear to me
Let these words fall upon us:

'O time! Suspend your flight and you, propitious
hours,
Suspend your too quick course:
Allow us now, please, to savour the rapid delights
Of our most beautiful days!
Enough unhappy ones here below implore you,
Flow, flow quickly for them;
Take away their days and the cares devouring
them;
Forget the happy ones.

But in vain I ask for some few, brief moments more,
Time escapes me and flies;
I say to this night: move more slowly! And the dawn
Comes to dispel the night.

Adrian Ludwig Richter, *Crossing the Elbe at Aussig*, 1837.
Oil on canvas, 116.5 x 156.5 cm. Gemäldegalerie, Dresden.

John Robert Cozens, *Lake Albano and Castel Gandolfo.*
Watercolour on paper. Leeds Museums and Galleries, Leeds.

Let's love, thus, let us love! For this fugitive hour
Let's hasten, let's rejoice!
For man has no port, time has no shore:
It flows and we pass by.'

Jealous time, can it be that these drunken moments
In which love pours its happiness on us in long
waves,
That these fly far away from us at the same speed
As unhappy days?

And so, can we not hold to the least trace of them?
What! Gone forever! What! All entirely lost!
This time that gave us those days, this time that
erases them
Will give us them no more!

Eternity, nothingness, dark abyss,
What do you make of all the days that you engulf?
Speak: will you give us back these sublime ecstasies
That you ravish from us?

O Lake, mute rocks and grottoes, obscuring forest!
You who time spares or whom it can rejuvenate,
Keep of this dark night, beautiful nature, keep
At least the memory!
Let it be in your repose, even in your storms,
Beautiful lake, in the look of your laughing hills,
In these dark firs, and in the savage stones
That lean out over you.

Let it be in the breeze that shivers and passes,
In the sounds of your shores echoing on your
shores,
In the silver browed star that whitens your surface
With its soft clarities.

Let the wind that softly moans and the reed that
sighs,
Let the high heady perfume of your balmy air,
And let everything that one hears, or sees, or
breathes,
Say out loud: they have loved!

Percy Bysshe Shelley
(1792-1822)

Alastor or the Spirit of Solitude

Earth, Ocean, Air, beloved brotherhood!
If our great Mother has imbued my soul
With aught of natural piety to feel
Your love, and recompense the boon with mine;
If dewy morn, and odorous noon, and even,
With sunset and its gorgeous ministers,
And solemn midnight's tingling silentness;
If autumn's hollow sighs in the sere wood,
And winter robing with pure snow and crowns
Of starry ice the grey grass and bare boughs;
If spring's voluptuous pantings when she breathes
Her first sweet kisses, have been dear to me;
If no bright bird, insect, or gentle beast
I consciously have injured, but still loved
And cherished these my kindred; then forgive
This boast, beloved brethren, and withdraw
No portion of your wonted favour now!

Mother of this unfathomable world!
Favour my solemn song, for I have loved
Thee ever, and thee only; I have watched
Thy shadow, and the darkness of thy steps,
And my heart ever gazes on the depth
Of thy deep mysteries. I have made my bed
In charnels and on coffins, where black death
Keeps record of the trophies won from thee,

Hoping to still these obstinate questionings
Of thee and thine, by forcing some lone ghost,
Thy messenger, to render up the tale
Of what we are. In lone and silent hours,
When night makes a weird sound of its own
stillness,
Like an inspired and desperate alchymist
Staking his very life on some dark hope,
Have I mixed awful talk and asking looks
With my most innocent love, until strange tears,
Uniting with those breathless kisses, made
Such magic as compels the charmed night
To render up thy charge:...and, though ne'er yet
Thou hast unveiled thy inmost sanctuary,
Enough from incommunicable dream,
And twilight phantasms, and deep noon-day
thought,
Has shone within me, that serenely now
And moveless, as a long-forgotten lyre
Suspended in the solitary dome
Of some mysterious and deserted fane,
I wait thy breath, Great Parent, that my strain
May modulate with murmurs of the air,
And motions of the forests and the sea,
And voice of living beings, and woven hymns
Of night and day, and the deep heart of man.

Karl Friedrich Schinkel, *Medieval City on a River,* 1815.
Oil on canvas, 95 x 140.6 cm. Nationalgalerie, Berlin.

Henry Fuseli, *Titania and Bottom,* c. 1790.
Oil on canvas, 217.2 x 275.6 cm. Tate Gallery, London.

John Keats
(1795-1821)

Poems

I stood tip-toe upon a little hill,
The air was cooling, and so very still.
That the sweet buds which with a modest pride
Pull droopingly, in slanting curve aside,
Their scantly leaved, and finely tapering stems,
Had not yet lost those starry diadems
Caught from the early sobbing of the morn.
The clouds were pure and white as flocks new shorn,
And fresh from the clear brook; sweetly they slept
On the blue fields of heaven, and then there crept
A little noiseless noise among the leaves,
Born of the very sigh that silence heaves:
For not the faintest motion could be seen
Of all the shades that slanted o'er the green.

There was wide wand'ring for the greediest eye,
To peer about upon variety;
Far round the horizon's crystal air to skim,
And trace the dwindled edgings of its brim;
To picture out the quaint, and curious bending
Of a fresh woodland alley, never ending;
Or by the bowery clefts, and leafy shelves,
Guess were the jaunty streams refresh themselves.
I gazed awhile, and felt as light, and free
As though the fanning wings of Mercury
Had played upon my heels: I was light-hearted,
And many pleasures to my vision started;
So I straightway began to pluck a posey
Of luxuries bright, milky, soft and rosy.

James Pradier, *Sappho,* 1852.
Marble and gilding, h. : 118 cm. Musée d'Orsay, Paris.

François Rude, *The Neapolitan Fisher,* 1833.
Marble, 82 x 88 x 48 cm. Musée du Louvre, Paris.

Heinrich Heine

(1797-1856)

Intermezzo

There once was a knight so afflicted with care,
So silent, with cheeks white and haggard,
He stumbled and bumbled he didn't know where,
In a gloomy trance he staggered.
He was so wooden, so clumsy, so daft,
The flowers and maidens giggled and laughed
As they passed the blundering laggard.

He often sat home in the gloomiest nook,
With the world of men he had broken.
He stretched out his arms with a yearning look,
Yet never a word would be spoken.
But soon as the hour of midnight came round,
A singing and ringing would strangely resound.
A knock on the door was the token.

Then in glides his loved one, in shimmering clothes
Of sea foam mantling her graces;
She flows and glows like a blossoming rose,
Her veil is of jewelled laces.
Her golden hair flutters around her pale form,
Her sweet eyes invite him, passionate, warm,
They fall in each other's embraces.

The knight holds her fast to his heart that aches,
The wooden one now burns in fire;
The pale one reddens, the dreamer awakes,
The shy one's passion mounts higher.
But she – she roguishly teases instead,
She lightly enwinds around his head
Her jewelled white veil of desire.

Then away to a palace of glass undersea
The magic spell carries him thither.
Near blind with the brightness and brilliancy
He stares in bewilderment with her.
The naiad embraces him loving-eyed,
The night is the bridegroom, the naiad the bride,
Her maidens play on the zither,

They play and they sing – so sweetly they sing! –
They dance and the air's so aromatic.
The knight feels his senses shattering,
And closer he clasps her, ecstatic…
Then all of a sudden the scene goes black:
Once more alone, the knight finds himself back
In his gloomy poet's attic.

Francesco Hayez, *The Kiss,* 1859.
Oil on canvas, 112 x 88 cm. Pinacoteca di Brera, Milan.

Alfred de Vigny
(1797-1863)

Chatterton

Act III, scene 1

He is sitting at the bottom of his bed and is writing on his knees. – For sure she doesn't love me. – And I want to stop thinking about it. – My hands are frozen and my head is burning. – Here I am facing my work alone. – It is not about smiling and being good, about greeting and shaking hands anymore! All that comedy is over: I'm starting another one with myself. – Now I need my will to be powerful enough to grab my soul and take it in turn into the corpse of characters brought back to life by me recalling them and into the ghosts of those that I create! Or else, in front of Chatterton who is ill, Chatterton who is cold and hungry, I need my will to place another Chatterton pretentiously, a Chatterton adorned for the pleasure of the audience and the latter be described by the former: the troubadour by the beggar. Here are the two possible kinds of poetry, that is all that there is! Entertain the audience or make them feel sorry for you; have some miserable puppets acting or be one oneself and make business of these antics! Open one's heart and make a show of it! And if it is wounded all the better! That makes it more precious; people buy it a higher price if it is even slightly mutilated!

(Standing up)

Stand up, creature of God, made in his own image, and admire yourself even in such condition!

(He laughs and sits back again. – An old clock strikes half an hour, two chimes.)

No, no! Time is warning; sit down and work, poor man! You waste your time whilst thinking: there is only one thought to have and it is that you are a poor man. – Do you hear? A poor man!

Friedrich Georg Kersting, *Caspar David Friedrich in his Studio,* 1812.
Oil on canvas, 51 x 40 cm. Nationalgalerie, Berlin.

Victor Hugo
(1802-1885)

Hernani

Act II, scene 4

HERNANI, DOÑA SOL

DOÑA SOL (grabbing Hernani's hand)
Now let us fly together quickly.

HERNANI

(pushing her back with a soft seriousness)
It well becomes you, loved one, in the trial hour to
prove
Thus strong, unchangeable, and willing even
To the end and depth of all to cling to me.
A noble wish, worthy a faithful soul!
But thou, O God, dost see that to accept
The joy that to my cavern she would bring
The treasure of a beauty that a king
Now covets – and that Doña Sol to me
Should all belong – that she with me should 'bide,
And all our lives be joined – this should be
Without regret, remorse – it is too late.
The scaffold is too near.

DOÑA SOL
What are you saying?

HERNANI
This king, whom to his face just now I braved
Will punish me for having dared to show
Him mercy. He already, perhaps, has reached
His palace, and is calling round his guards
And servants, his great lords, his headsmen…

DOÑA SOL
Hernani! Oh I shudder.
So let us be quick then and fly together.

HERNANI
Together! No, the hour has passed for that.
Alas! When to my eyes thou didst reveal
Thyself, so good and generous, deigning even
To love me with a helpful love, I could
But offer you – I, wretched one! – the hills,

Ary Scheffer, *The Ghosts of Paolo and Francesca Appear to Dante and Virgil,* 1854.
Oil on canvas, 57.7 x 81.3 cm. Hamburger Kunsthalle, Hamburg.

William Blake, *Pity*, c. 1795.
Watercolour and ink on paper, 42.5 x 53.9 cm. Tate Gallery, London.

The woods, the torrents, bread of the proscribed,
The bed of turf, all that the forest gives;
Thy pity then emboldened me, but now
To ask of thee to share the scaffold! No,
No, Doña Sol. That is for me alone.

DOÑA SOL
And yet you promised even that!

HERNANI (falling on his knees)
At this same moment, when perchance from out
The shadow Death approaches, to wind up
All mournfully a life of mournfulness,
I do declare that here a man proscribed,
Enduring trouble great, profound – and rock'd
In blood-stained cradle – black as is the gloom
Which spreads over all my life, I still declare
I am happy, to-be-envied man,
For you have loved me, and your love have owned!
For you have whispered blessings on my brow accursed!

DOÑA SOL (bent over his head)
Hernani!

HERNANI
Praised by the fate
Sweet and propitious that for me now sets
This flower upon the precipice's brink!

(raising himself)
'Tis not to you that I am speaking thus,
It is to Heaven that hears and unto God.

DOÑA SOL
Let me go with you.

HERNANI
Ah! It would be a crime
To pluck the flower while falling in the abyss.
Go: I have breathed the perfume. 'Tis enough.
Remould your life, by me so sadly marred.
This old man wed; 'tis I release you now.
To darkness I return. Be happy thou –
Be happy and forget.

DOÑA SOL
No, I will have my portion of thy shroud!
I follow thee and I hang upon thy steps.

HERNANI (pressing her in his arms)
Oh, let me go
Alone!

(He quits her with a convulsive movement and goes)

DOÑA SOL (mournfully, and clasping her hands)
Hernani! You fly from me! Mad woman,
You've given up your life to only see yourself turned away
And, after so much love and trouble,
Not even to have the happiness to die by his side!

HERNANI
Exiled, proscribed, a fearful man I am!

Aurore Dupin, Baroness Dudevant, called George Sand
(1804–1876)

The Devil's Pool

The Plough

For a long time I had been gazing in deep melancholy at Holbein's labourer, and now I was walking in the country, ruminating on the life of the soil and the fate of the man who cultivates it. It must be dismal indeed to spend all your strength and all your days in furrowing the breast of this jealous earth, struggling to wrest from it the treasures of its fertility, when at the end of the day the only profit and the only reward for such hard labour is a piece of the coarsest and blackest bread. These rides which cover the ground, these harvests, these fruit, these proud cattle fattening in the lush grass – they are the property of a few, for the majority merely the instruments of toil and slavery. In general the man of leisure loves for their own sake neither the fields and meadows, nor the beauties of nature, nor the magnificent beasts which exist merely in order to be turned into pieces of gold for his use. He comes into the country in search of fresh air and health, but, after a brief stay, away he goes again to spend the fruit of his vassals' labours in the big towns.

As for the working man, he is too oppressed, too wretched, too afraid of the future, to enjoy the beauties of the countryside and the charms of rustic life. For him also the golden fields, the fair meadows and the magnificent beasts represent bags of money – in which he will have but a miserable share, insufficient for his needs: but all the same he must fill them every year, these damned bags, to satisfy his master and earn the right to live a life of penury and misery on his land.

John Crome, *The Poringland Chestnut*, c. 1818-1820.
Oil on canvas, 125.1 x 100.3 cm. Tate Gallery, London.

Yet nature herself is perpetually young, lovely and generous, liberally bestowing her poetry and beauty on all creatures and all plants which are allowed to go freely. She has the key to happiness, which no one has ever been able to steal from her. The happiest man in the world would be the labourer who had real skill and full understanding of his work, so that in the intelligent use of his strength he achieved both physical well-being and a sense of liberty; and who still had the time to allow his heart and his mind to play a part in his life – understanding his own work, and loving the work of God.

The artist enjoys this sort of pleasure in contemplating and reproducing the beauties of nature, but his enjoyment will be marred if he is a man of feeling, by the misery of the people who inhabit this earthly paradise. True happiness would be where mind, heart and hand worked together under the eye of Providence: God's munificence and the delight of the human soul in holy harmony. Then, instead of the pitiful and terrible figure of Death walking, whip in hand, along the labourer's furrow, the painter of allegories could show beside him a radiant angel scattering generous handfuls of blessed corn over the steaming earth.

And the dream of a sweet, free, poetic, industrious and simple life for the man of the soil is not so far-fetched as to be dismissed as a fantasy. Virgil's sweet, sad words: 'O happy man of soil, did he but know his happiness!' are a lament, but, like other laments they are also a prediction. A day will come when the labourer can also be an artist – if not to express (which by then will be unimportant) at least to appreciate beauty. Does he not already have, in the form of instinctive feelings and vague dreams, the beginnings of that mysterious intuition which is poetry?

Those who are protected by some measure of well-being, whose moral and intelligent development is not entirely stifled by too great a misery, are already on the first step towards true, pure and conscious happiness. And besides, if the voice of poetry has been raised before now from the midst of weariness and suffering, why should we suppose spirited life to be incompatible with manual labour? Certainly it is not usually compatible with excessive work and extreme poverty, but let no one say that when all the men do no more than a reasonable amount of work we shall have nothing but bad workers and bad poets. Any man who derives noble enjoyment from the sentiments of poetry is a true poet, even if he has never written a verse in his life.

Carl Blechen, *In the Park of the Villa d'Este,* 1831-1832.
Oil on canvas, 127.5 x 94 cm. Schloss Charlottenburg, Potsdam.

Auguste Préault, *Virgil*, 1853.
Bronze with a brown patina, 95 x 85.5 x 23 cm. Musée d'Orsay, Paris.

Auguste Préault, *Dante,* 1852.
Bronze with a brown patina, 95 x 85.9 x 23 cm. Musée d'Orsay, Paris.

Alfred de Musset
(1810-1857)

The Confession of a Child of the Century

There were three elements in the life offered to young people at that time: behind them, there was a past gone forever, still moving on its ruins with all the fossils of centuries of absolutism; in front of them, a dawn with an immense horizon, the first lights of the future; and between those worlds…there was something like the ocean that separates the old continent from young America, a vague and floating je-ne-sais-quoi, a stormy sea full of shipwrecks with, from time to time, some faraway white sail or some steam boat crossing. In a nutshell, between those worlds, there was the present century which separates the past from the future, which is neither one nor the other but looks like both at the same time and where at each step that one takes one does not know whether one is walking on a seed or a piece of debris.

This is the chaotic context in which one had to make choices then; and that was what strong and bold young people, who were heirs to the Empire and the Revolution, had to face. However, they would not have anything to do with the past but they loved the future, like Pygmalion loved Galatea: for them it was like a lover made of marble and they were waiting for it to come to life, in the flesh.

Léon Cogniet, *Scene of the Massacre of the Innocents,* 1824.
Oil on canvas, 265 x 235 cm. Musée des Beaux-Arts de Rennes, Rennes.

Hubert Robert, *Demolition of the Bastille,* 1789.
Oil on canvas, 77 x 114 cm. Musée Carnavalet – musée d'Histoire de Paris, Paris.

So they were left with the present, the spirit of the century, which was an angel of dusk that neither belongs to night nor daytime; they found it sitting on a bag of lime full of bones, ill at ease in the coat of selfish people and shivering. At the sight of this spectre who was half a mummy and half a foetus, their soul started to be distressed by the idea of death; they approached it like a traveller who is shown the daughter of an old count of Sarvenden in Strasbourg; she is embalmed wearing the costume of a bride: that childish skeleton makes one shudder for it wears the ring of marriage on a slender white hand but its head crumbles into dust amid orange blossoms.

Like when a storm is about to break, there are strong winds passing through the forests and making the trees rustle. Then, there is a deep silence; in the same way Napoleon had shaken the world; kings had felt their crowns wobbling on their heads and in trying to hold them in place they had only felt that their hair stood on its ends in terror. The pope had travelled three hundred miles to bless him in the name of God and crown him but Napoleon had taken it from the pope's hands and crowned himself. So everything had trembled in gloomy old Europe. Then there had been silence. An inexpressible feeling of general discomfort started to develop in all young hearts. Forced to inaction by all the monarchs in the world and condemned to idleness and boredom, young people saw the foamy waves against which they had prepared themselves going away. All these gladiators ready for fighting felt deeply miserable. The richest turned to a dissolute lifestyle; the less rich took a position and resigned themselves to be part of the Church or the army; the poor threw themselves in enthusiasm for the sake of it, in empty great concepts and in the horrible sea of pointless action. As human weakness does not like being on its own and as men are gregarious by nature, politics got involved. One would fight guards on the steps of the parliament or run to a play where Talma was wearing a wig that made him look like Caesar; one would rush to the funeral of a liberal MP. However, on both sides, there was not anyone who, once at home, did not feel bitterly useless.

[...] Do not get it wrong: the black clothes that the men of our time wear are a dreadful symbol; to get to that point, it has been necessary to get rid of every single piece of armour and every ornament. It is human rationality that broke all illusions, but it is mourning and asks for consolation.

Mikhail Yuryevich Lermontov
(1814-1841)

A Hero of Our Time

Book I: Bela

The Heart of a Russian

Chapter I

I was travelling post from Tiflis.

All the luggage I had in my cart consisted of one small portmanteau half filled with travelling-notes on Georgia; of these the greater part has been lost, fortunately for you; but the portmanteau itself and the rest of its contents have remained intact, fortunately for me.

As I entered the Koishaur Valley the sun was disappearing behind the snow-clad ridge of the mountains. In order to accomplish the ascent of Mount Koishaur by nightfall, my driver, an Ossete, urged on the horses indefatigably, singing zealously the while at the top of his voice.

What a glorious place that valley is! On every hand are inaccessible mountains, steep, yellow slopes scored by water-channels, and reddish rocks draped with green ivy and crowned with clusters of plane-trees. Yonder, at an immense height, is the golden fringe of the snow. Down below rolls the River Aragva, which, after bursting noisily forth from the dark and misty depths of the gorge, with an unnamed stream clasped in its embrace, stretches out like a thread of silver, its waters glistening like a snake with flashing scales. Arrived at the foot of Mount Koishaur, we stopped at a dukhan. About a score of Georgians and mountaineers were gathered there in a noisy crowd, and, close by, a caravan of camels had halted for the night. I was obliged to hire oxen to drag my cart up that accursed mountain, as it was now autumn and the roads were slippery with ice.

Thomas Cole, *The Departure,* 1837.
Oil on canvas, 100.3 x 160 cm. Corcoran Gallery of Art, Washington, D.C.

Joseph Mallord William Turner, *Dido building Carthage; or, the Rise of the Carthaginian Empire*, 1815.
Oil on canvas, 155.5 x 232 cm. The National Gallery, London.

Major Artists

Hubert Robert, *Alexander the Great Visiting the Tomb of Achilles,* 1755-1760.
Oil on canvas, 63 x 48 cm. Private collection.

Hubert Robert, *Landscape with Architecture and a Canal,* 1783.
Oil on canvas, 129 x 182.5 cm. The State Hermitage Museum, St Petersburg.

Hubert Robert
(Paris, 1733-1808)

Hubert Robert was the son of a Nicolas Robert, who worked in the Marquis of Choiseul-Stainville's household, a connection that was helpful to Hubert throughout his life. From 1751 to 1754 he studied under the French sculptor Michel-Ange Slodtz, who in fact encouraged him to paint. He then left for Rome at the age of twenty-one, where he stayed for eleven years, at first joining the French Academy. There he spent time with Piranesi's circle, taking much influence from the Italian artist's etchings of Rome, and executed many outdoor sketches of ruins and Roman buildings. The contrast between the ruins of ancient Rome and his own time excited his keenest interest and, although he had started for Italy independently, the credit he there acquired procured him the protection of the minister Marigny and an official allowance. During this time he became acquainted with the Abbé de Saint-Non, who would later produce many engravings of his work, and who took Robert and the artist Jean-Honoré Fragonard on a trip to Naples and Pompeii.

In 1765 Robert returned to Paris to meet with great success. He first exhibited his work in the Salon of 1767, and it was extremely well received. He became known as "Robert-les-ruines" for his depictions of romantically-lit ruins set in idealised surroundings, some of which were imaginary, such as his *View of the Great Gallery in the Louvre in Ruins* (1796), but many of which were based on direct observational sketches. His incessant activity as an artist, his daring character and his many adventures attracted general sympathy and admiration. In the fourth canto of his *L'Imagination*, Jacques Delille celebrated Robert's miraculous escape when lost in the Catacombs; later in life, when imprisoned during the Terror and marked for the guillotine, through a fatal accident another died in his place and Robert lived. Robert eventually died of apoplexy on the 15th April 1808.

This French artist deserves to be remembered not so much for his skill as a painter as for the liveliness and focus with which he treated the subjects he painted. The quantity of his work is immense: the Louvre alone contains over two hundred works by his hand and specimens are frequently to be met with in provincial museums and private collections. Robert's work has a scenic quality that brought about his selection by Voltaire to paint the decorations of his theatre at Ferney. In Italy his work was frequently reproduced by Liénard amongst others.

Henry Fuseli, *The Nightmare*, 1781.
Oil on canvas, 101.6 x 126.7 cm. Detroit Institute of Fine Arts, Detroit.

Johann Heinrich Füssli, called Henry Fuseli
(Zürich 1741 – London 1825)

An English painter and writer on art, of German-Swiss family, Fuseli was born in Zürich in Switzerland on the 7th February 1741. His father was John Caspar Füssli, a painter. Fuseli's father intended him for the church, and with this view sent him to the Caroline college of his native town, where he received an excellent classical education.

After taking orders in 1761 Fuseli was obliged to leave his country in consequence of having aided the exposure of an unjust magistrate, whose family was still powerful enough to make its vengeance felt. He first travelled through Germany and then, in 1765, visited England, where he supported himself for some time with writing. He became acquainted with Sir Joshua Reynolds, to whom he showed his drawings. On Sir Joshua's advice he then devoted himself wholly to art. In 1770 he made an artistic pilgrimage to Italy, where he remained till 1778, changing his name from Füssli to Fuseli, as it sounded more Italian. Early in 1779 he returned to England via Zürich. He found a commission awaiting him from an Alderman Boydell, who was then organising his celebrated Shakespeare gallery. Fuseli painted a number of pieces for this patron.

In 1788 Fuseli married Sophia Rawlins, and he soon after became an Associate of the Royal Academy. Later he was promoted to the grade of Academician, then Professor and Keeper. In 1799 he exhibited a series of paintings inspired by the works of Milton, with a view to forming a Milton gallery similar to Boydell's Shakespeare gallery. This exhibition, which closed in 1800, proved a failure as regards profit.

The sculptor Canova, when on his visit to England, was much taken with Fuseli's works, and on returning to Rome in 1817 caused him to be elected a member of the first class of the Academy of St. Luke. Fuseli, after a life of uninterrupted good health, died at Putney Hill, London, on the 16th April 1825, at the advanced age of eighty-four, and was buried in the crypt of St Paul's Cathedral. He was comparatively rich at his death, though his professional gains had always appeared to be meagre.

Henry Fuseli, *The Nightmare*, 1790-1791.
Oil on canvas, 76 x 63 cm. Goethe-Museum, Frankfurt am Main.

As a painter, Fuseli was inventive and original and ever aspiring to the highest forms of excellence. His mind was capable of grasping and realising the loftiest conceptions, which, however, he often spoilt on the canvas by exaggerating the proportions, and throwing his figures into attitudes of fantastic and over-strained contortion. He delighted in the supernatural and idealised his compositions, believing a certain amount of exaggeration necessary in historical painting. "Damn Nature! she always puts me out," was his characteristic exclamation. In this theory he was confirmed by the study of Michelangelo's works and the marble statues of the Monte Cavallo. But this idea was carried out to excess by him. A striking illustration of this occurs in his picture of *Hamlet and the Ghost*: Hamlet, it has been said, looks as if he would burst his clothes with convulsive cramps in his muscles.

On the other hand, his paintings are never languid or cold. His figures are full of life, earnestness and intense purpose. Like Rubens he excelled in the art of setting his figures in motion. Though the lofty and terrible was his proper sphere, Fuseli had fine perception of the ludicrous. The grotesque humour of his fairy scenes, especially those from *A Midsummer Night's Dream*, is in its way not less remarkable than the poetic power of his more ambitious works. As a colourist Fuseli has but small claims to distinction. He scorned to set a palette as most artists do; he merely dashed his tints recklessly over it. This recklessness may perhaps be explained by the fact that he did not paint in oil until he was twenty-five years of age. Despite these drawbacks he possessed the elements of a great painter.

Fuseli painted more than two hundred pictures, but he exhibited only a minority of them. His first painting to excite particular attention was the *Nightmare*, exhibited in 1782. His sketches or designs number about eight hundred; they have admirable qualities of invention and design, and are frequently superior to his paintings.

Henry Fuseli, *Titania and Bottom,* 1793-1794.
Oil on canvas, 169 x 135 cm. Kunsthaus, Zürich.

Francisco de Goya y Lucientes, *The Clothed Maja*, 1800-1803.
Oil on canvas, 97 x 190 cm. Museo Nacional del Prado, Madrid.

Francisco de Goya y Lucientes, *The Swing*, 1779.
Oil on canvas, 260 x 165 cm. Museo Nacional del Prado, Madrid.

Francisco de Goya y Lucientes
(Fuendetodos, 1746 – Bordeaux, 1828)

Goya is perhaps the most approachable of painters. His art, like his life, is an open book. He concealed nothing from his contemporaries, and offered his art to them with the same frankness. The entrance to his world is not barricaded with technical difficulties. He proved that if a man has the capacity to live and multiply his experiences, to fight and work, he can produce great art without classical decorum and traditional respectability. He was born in 1746, in Fuendetodos, a small Spanish mountain village of a hundred inhabitants. As a child he worked in the fields with his two brothers and his sister until his talent for drawing put an end to his misery. At fourteen, supported by a wealthy patron, he went to Saragossa to study with a court painter and later, when he was nineteen, on to Madrid.

Up to his thirty-seventh year, if we leave out of account the tapestry cartoons of unheralded decorative quality and five small pictures, Goya painted nothing of any significance, but once in control of his refractory powers, he produced masterpieces with the speed of Rubens. His court appointment was followed by a decade of incessant activity – years of painting and scandal, with intervals of bad health.

Goya's etchings demonstrate a draughtsmanship of the first rank. In paint, like Velázquez, he is more or less dependent on the model, but not in the detached fashion of the expert in still-life. If a woman was ugly, he made her a despicable horror; if she was alluring, he dramatised her charm. He preferred to finish his portraits at one sitting and was a tyrant with his models. Like Velázquez too, he concentrated on faces, but he drew his heads cunningly, and constructed them out of tones of transparent greys. Monstrous forms inhabit his black-and-white world; these are his most profoundly deliberated productions. His fantastic figures, as he called them, fill us with a sense of ignoble joy, aggravate our devilish instincts and delight us with the uncharitable ecstasies of destruction. His genius attained its highest point in his etchings on the horrors of war. When placed beside the work of Goya, other pictures of war pale into sentimental studies of cruelty. He avoided the scattered action of the battlefield, and confined himself to isolated scenes of butchery. Nowhere else did he display such mastery of form and movement, such dramatic gestures and appalling effects of light and darkness. In all directions Goya renewed and innovated.

Francisco de Goya y Lucientes, *The Nude Maja*, 1797-1800.
Oil on canvas, 98 x 191 cm. Museo Nacional del Prado, Madrid.

John Robert Cozens, *View of a Castle between Bolzano and Trent,* 18th century.
Watercolour on canvas. Victoria & Albert Museum, London.

John Robert Cozens, *View from Mirabella,* c. 1782.
Watercolour, 25 x 37.4 cm. Victoria & Albert Museum, London.

John Robert Cozens
(London, 1752-1797)

As the son of the Russian-born watercolourist Alexander Cozens, is it not surprising that John Robert Cozens exhibited some early works with the Society of Artists at the age of fifteen. He was taught by his father, and between 1776 and 1779 he travelled in Switzerland and Italy with the scholar and connoisseur Richard Payne Knight, painting many watercolour Alpine views and Italian landscapes such as *A Cavern in the Campagna, Rome* (in the Victoria & Albert Museum). He returned to England in 1779 and lived in Bath, where he enjoyed some success with the works he had executed on the continent, making and selling numerous copies. He travelled again to Italy in 1782 with the writer (and later politician) William Beckford, who was then one of his patrons. Cozens made many sketches during the trip, which came to an end when an outbreak of malaria struck the party, including the artist himself. He recovered in Portici in the home of Sir William Hamilton, a British diplomat.

From 1793 Cozens began to suffer from severe mental illness, and had a breakdown in 1794 which resulted in him being placed in the care of a Dr Thomas Monro for the last few years of his life. This doctor made several of Cozens' works available for study by art students, which had great influence on such artists as J. M. W. Turner and Thomas Girtin. Cozens was buried in London on New Year's Day 1798.

Cozens' works are filled with a quiet majesty and a sense of vastness. The painter John Constable described Cozens as "the greatest genius that ever touched landscape", and stated that his watercolours were "all poetry". Henry Fuseli professed that he "saw with an enchanted eye, and drew with an enchanted hand."[1] Indeed, the nuances of light and colour and the illusionistic impression of the scenes create an atmosphere of mystery. This evocation of mood in watercolour paintings demonstrates the huge development in the medium that occurred around the time, and highlights the idea, then a relatively new one, that landscapes could inspire emotion in a way that had previously been reserved for history painting.

William Blake, Plate from *Jerusalem, The Emanation of the Giant Albion*, 1804.
Etching and watercolour. Yale Center for British Art, New Haven.

William Blake
(London, 1757-1827)

Poet, draughtsman, engraver and painter. William Blake's work is made up of several elements – Gothic art, Germanic reverie, the Bible, Milton and Shakespeare – to which were added Dante and a certain taste for linear designs resembling geometric diagrams, and relates him to the great classical movement inspired by Winckelmann and propagated by David. This is the sole point of contact discernible between the classicism of David and English art, though furtive and indirect. Blake is the most mystic of the English painters, perhaps the only true mystic. He was ingenious in his inner imagination, and his interpretations of ancient and modern poets reveal as true and candid a spirit as the title of his first work – poems he composed, illustrated and set to music, *Songs of Innocence and of Experience*. Later he achieved grandeur, power and profundity, especially in certain tempera paintings. Like others, Blake was considered an eccentric by most of his contemporaries, until his genius was recognised in the second half of the nineteenth century.

Blake was born in Soho in London, the city in which he lived his whole life – excepting a brief period spent in Sussex – and which influenced his ideas of good and evil. He left school at the age of ten to attend the Henry Pars Drawing Academy. At fifteen he finished his education at the academy, and became apprentice to the engraver James Basire. Blake's official profession was that of an engraver; it is said that he could not afford an apprenticeship to a painter. Painting and writing he did for pleasure. His apprenticeship lasted six years, after which he joined the Royal Academy of Art. He opened his own shop in 1784, and it was just prior to this that his friends paid for his poems to be published in a volume called *Poetical Sketches*; Blake had been writing poetry since the age of thirteen. The title demonstrates the uniting of different arts, here poetry and drawing, that was a fundamental feature of Romanticism. In his later publications, Blake illustrated his poems with evocative and sometimes almost grotesque imagery, aided by his wife Catherine Boucher, whom he married in 1782. Blake was preoccupied with ideas of good and evil, which was manifest in his work. He hated slavery and abhorred the conditions and inequality of eighteenth-century London life, which he described in his illustrated poem *London*.

Blake died in 1827 at the age of sixty-nine. After his death and that of his wife, some parts of his work, both writing and imagery, that were deemed too political, heretical or sexual were destroyed or erased by various parties.

William Blake, *The Genius of Shakespeare,* 1809.
Feather and watercolour on paper, 30.8 x 19.1 cm. The British Museum, London.

Antoine Jean Gros, *Napoleon Bonaparte on Arcole Bridge, November 17, 1796,* 1796.
Oil on canvas, 130 x 94 cm. Musée national du château et des Trianons, Versailles.

Antoine Jean Gros, *Napoleon on the Battlefield of Eylau (February 9, 1807),* 1808.
Oil on canvas, 521 x 784 cm. Musée du Louvre, Paris.

Antoine Jean Gros, Baron **Gros**
(Paris, 1771-1835)

Gros's father, who was a miniaturist, began to teach him to draw at the age of six. Towards the end of 1785 Gros chose to enter Jacques-Louis David's studio, which he frequented assiduously, at the same time attending classes at the Collège Mazarin. In 1791, the death of his father, who had fallen on hard times during the Revolution, threw Gros upon his own resources. He now devoted himself wholly to his profession, and in 1792 competed for the *Grand Prix*, but was unsuccessful. About this time, however, on the recommendation of the École des beaux-arts, he was employed to paint the portraits of the members of the Convention. When the development of the Revolution meant that in 1793 Gros had to leave France for Italy, he supported himself in Genoa by the same means, producing a great quantity of miniatures. He visited Florence, and on returning to Genoa made the acquaintance of Josephine de Beauharnais, following her to Milan, where he was well-received by her husband. On the 15th November 1796, Gros was present with the army near Arcola when Bonaparte planted the tricolour on the bridge. Gros painted this moment, and showed from his treatment of it that he had found his vocation. Bonaparte at once gave him the post of "inspecteur aux revues", which enabled him to follow the army, and in 1797 the general nominated him to the commission charged with selecting the spoils which should enrich the Louvre.

In 1799, having escaped from the besieged city of Genoa, Gros made his way to Paris, and in the beginning of 1801 took up his quarters in the Capucins. His *esquisse* (Musée de Nantes) of the *Battle of Nazareth* won the prize offered in 1802 by the consuls, but he never received it, owing, it is said, to the jealousy Napoleon felt for Junot. However the First Consul made up for this by commissioning Gros to paint his own visit to the pesthouse of Jaffa. *Bonaparte visiting the Plague-Stricken in Jaffa (11th March 1799)* (Louvre) was followed by the *Battle of Akoubir, 25th July 1799* in 1806 (Versailles), and *Napoleon on the Field of the Battle of Eylau (9th February 1807)* in 1808 (Louvre). These three subjects – the popular leader facing the pestilence unmoved, challenging the splendid instant of victory, heart-sick with the bitter cost of a hard-won field – made Gros famous. Gros was decorated and named Baron of the Empire by Napoleon, after the Salon of 1808, and under the Restoration he became a professor at the École des beaux-arts and Chevalier of the order of St Michel. However, as the army and its general separated from the people, Gros, called on to illustrate episodes representative only of the fulfilment of personal ambition, ceased to find satisfaction in this employment of his genius. Trained in the style of the Classicists, he was shackled by their rules, even when – by his naturalistic treatment of subjects, and use of picturesque effect in colour and tone – he seemed to run counter to them. In 1810 his *Capitulation of Madrid, 4th December 1808* and *Battle of the Pyramids, 21st July 1798* (Versailles) show that his star had deserted him. His *Francis I and Charles V at the Abbey of Saint-Denis* of 1812 (Louvre) had considerable success, but the decoration of the dome of the church of St Geneviève (begun in 1811 and completed in 1824), now the Pantheon, is the only work of Gros's later years which shows his early force and vigour. The *Departure of Louis XVIII from the Palais des Tuileries, night of the 20th March 1815* (Versailles), the *Embarkation of the Duchess of Angoulême at Pouillac* (Bordeaux), the ceiling of the Egyptian room in the Louvre, and finally his *Hercules and Diomedes*, exhibited in 1835, demonstrate that Gros's efforts – in accordance with the advice of his old master, David – to stem the rising tide of Romanticism, served only to damage his once brilliant reputation. Exasperated by criticism and the consciousness of failure, Gros sought refuge in the unrefined. On the 25th June 1835 he was found drowned on the shores of the Seine near Sèvres. From a paper which he had placed in his hat it became known that *"las de la vie, et trahi par les dernières facultés qui la lui rendaient unsupportable, il avait résolu de s'en défaire"* ("tired of life, and betrayed by last faculties which rendered it bearable, he had resolved to end it").

Antoine Jean Gros, *Bonaparte Visiting the Plague House at Jaffa,* 1804.
Oil on canvas, 523 x 715 cm. Musée du Louvre, Paris.

Caspar David Friedrich, *The Tomb of Ulrich von Hutten,* 1824.
Oil on canvas, 93.5 x 73.4 cm. Staatliche Kunstsammlungen, Weimar.

Caspar David Friedrich, *The Cross in the Mountains,* 1808.
Oil on canvas, 115 x 110 cm. Gemäldegalerie, Dresden.

Caspar David Friedrich
(Greiswald, 1774 – Dresden, 1840)

Like Gainsborough, Friedrich is mostly known for his landscapes. They depict trees, hills, and misty mornings based on his observation of nature. Mountains symbolise an immovable faith while the trees are an allegory of hope. Therefore his landscapes reflect his spiritual relationship with nature and his religious aspirations. His *Monk by the Sea* expresses his recurring theme of the insignificance of the individual in relation to the vastness of nature. A draughtsman and printmaker as well as a painter, he was one of the greatest German leaders of Romanticism.

Friedrich was born into a strict Lutheran family and was to a great extent self-taught. He studied at the Academy in Copenhagen between 1794 and 1798 before moving to Dresden, where he met Philipp Otto Runge, another significant German Romantic painter. His early works were in watercolour or ink, but at a later stage he moved on to oil painting, probably not until after the age of thirty. He depicted the landscapes of northern Germany, closely observing the light and atmosphere of this particular environment. He painted one of his most controversial works in 1808, *The Cross in the Mountains,* an altarpiece showing a cross rising out of a rocky peak surrounded by trees, almost silhouetted against an evening sky, the setting sun's rays forming a natural halo. Never before had an altarpiece been a simple landscape.

One of Friedrich's most famous paintings, and the one that seems to most remind viewers of the essence of Romanticism, is of course *The Wanderer above the Sea of Fog,* painted in 1818. A man stands on a rocky peak, his back to the viewer, gazing out at a sea of cloud. Mountains loom out of the mist, and the feeling of awe inspired by the power of nature was characteristic of the sublime aspect central to Romanticism. In 1835 Friedrich suffered a stroke, which resulted in a paralysis that meant he could never paint again, and he died five years later.

Caspar David Friedrich,
Woman in Morning Light, 1818.
Oil on canvas, 22 x 30.5 cm.
Museum Folkwang, Essen.

Joseph Mallord William Turner, *The Burning of the Houses of Lords and Commons,*
October 16, 1834, c. 1834-1835. Oil on canvas, 92.1 x 123.2 cm. Philadelphia Museum of Art, Philadelphia.

Joseph Mallord William Turner
(London, 1775-1851)

At fifteen, Turner was already exhibiting his *View of Lambeth.* He soon acquired the reputation of an immensely clever watercolourist. A disciple of Girtin and Cozens, he showed in his choice and presentation of theme a picturesque imagination which seemed to mark him out for a brilliant career as an illustrator. He travelled, first in his native land and then on several occasions in France, the Rhine Valley, Switzerland and Italy. He soon began to look beyond illustration. However, even in works in which we are tempted to see only picturesque imagination, there appears his dominant and guiding ideal of lyric landscape. His choice of a single master from the past is an eloquent witness, for he studied profoundly such canvases of Claude as he could find in England, copying and imitating them with a marvellous degree of perfection. His cult for the great painter never failed. He desired his *Sun rising through Vapour* and *Dido building Carthage* to be placed in the National Gallery side by side with two of Claude's masterpieces. And there we may still see them and judge how legitimate was this proud and splendid homage.

It was only in 1819 that Turner went to Italy, to go again in 1829 and 1840. Certainly Turner experienced emotions and found subjects for reverie there which he later translated in terms of his own genius into symphonies of light and colour. Ardour is tempered with melancholy, as shadow strives with light. Melancholy, even as it appears in the enigmatic and profound creation of Albrecht Dürer, finds no home in Turner's protean fairyland – what place could it have in a cosmic dream? Humanity does not appear there, except perhaps as stage characters at whom we hardly glance. Turner's pictures fascinate us and yet we think of nothing precise, nothing human, only unforgettable colours and phantoms that lay hold on our imaginations. Humanity really only inspired him when linked with the idea of death – a strange death, more a lyrical dissolution – like the finale of an opera.

Joseph Mallord William Turner, *South View of Salisbury Cathedral from the Cloister,* c. 1802.
Watercolour, 68 x 49.6 cm. Victoria & Albert Museum, London.

John Constable, *East Bergholt Church,* 19th century.
Oil on canvas. Private collection.

John Constable, *The Hay Wain,* 1821.
Oil on canvas, 130.2 x 185.4 cm. The National Gallery, London.

John Constable
(East Bergholt, 1776 – London, 1837)

John Constable was the first English landscape painter to take no lessons from the Dutch. He is instead indebted to the landscapes of Rubens, but his real model was Gainsborough, whose landscapes, with great trees planted in well-balanced masses on land sloping upwards towards the frame, have a rhythm often found in Rubens. Constable's originality does not lie in his choice of subjects, which frequently repeated themes beloved by Gainsborough.

Nevertheless, Constable seems to belong to a new century; he ushered in a new era. The difference in his approach results both from technique and feeling. Except for the French, Constable was the first landscape painter to consider as a primary and essential task the sketch made directly from nature at a single sitting; an idea which contains in essence the destinies of modern landscape, and perhaps of most modern painting. It is this momentary 'impression' of all the things which will be the soul of the future work. Working at leisure upon the large canvas, an artist's aim is to enrich and complete the sketch while retaining its pristine freshness. These are the two processes to which Constable devoted himself, while discovering the exuberant abundance of life in the simplest of country places. He had the palette of a creative colourist and a technique of vivid hatchings heralding that of the French Impressionists. He audaciously and frankly introduced green into painting, the green of lush meadows, the green of summer foliage, all the greens which, until then, painters had refused to see except through bluish, yellow, or – more often – brown spectacles.

Of the great landscape painters who occupied so important a place in nineteenth-century art, Corot was probably the only one to escape the influence of Constable. All the others are more or less direct descendants of the master of East Bergholt.

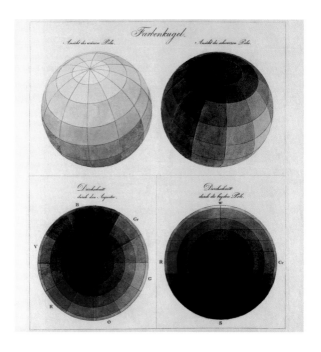

Philipp Otto Runge, *Farbenkugel (Colour Sphere)*, 1809.
Engraving painted with watercolours, 22.5 x 18.9 cm. Hamburger Kunsthalle, Hamburg.

Philipp Otto Runge, *Morning* (first version), 1808.
Oil on canvas, 108.9 x 85.4 cm. Hamburger Kunsthalle, Hamburg.

Philipp Otto Runge
(Walgast, 1777 – Hamburg, 1810)

The German Romantic painter Runge moved from his hometown to Hamburg at the age of eighteen, where he worked for his brother Daniel. His brother later gave him an allowance so that he could practise his art as he wanted. Runge studied painting in Hamburg and later at the Copenhagen Academy before moving to Dresden. There he met Caspar David Friedrich and the pair became friends. He married Pauline Bassenge in 1804, and the couple returned to Hamburg. Runge's major paintings were executed at this time, among them *The Nightingale's Lesson*, *Rest on the Flight into Egypt*, *The Artist's Parents*, *The Hülsenbeck Children* and two versions of *Morning*. As time went on, Runge moved away from history painting towards landscape painting, and he proved to be of great influence on the English Romanticists. He died young, at the age of just thirty-three, with his major work *Die Tageszeiten* (*Times of Day*) unfinished. This was a cycle of huge compositions which was designed to be hung in a particular architectural environment and viewed with poetry and music, which embodied the Romantic concept of *Gesamtkunstwerk* – "total art". The designs for this work were engraved in 1805, and were the only pieces by him really known to the public during his lifetime. Just before he died of tuberculosis he created *The Colour Sphere*, an extended and developed three-dimensional version of the colour wheel, which organised the colours by hue, brightness and saturation.

Théodore Géricault, *Officer of the Hussars,* 1812.
Oil on canvas, 349 x 266 cm. Musée du Louvre, Paris.

Théodore Géricault
(Rouen, 1791 – Paris 1824)

Jean Louis André Théodore Géricault, known more simply as Théodore Géricault, was born in Rouen in 1791. In 1808 he entered the studio of Charles Vernet, from where, in 1810, he moved to that of Guérin, whom he drove to despair with his passion for Rubens and the unorthodox manner in which he persisted in interpreting nature. At the Salon of 1812 Géricault attracted attention with his *Officer of the Hussars* (Louvre), a work in which he depicted the cavalry in the hour of its triumph, and demonstrated the solid training received from Guérin in rendering a picturesque point of view which was in itself a protest against the cherished convictions of the neoclassical school. Two years later, in 1814, he re-exhibited this work accompanied by the reverse picture, *The Wounded Cuirassier* (Louvre) and in both subjects drew attention to contemporary life, treated neglected types of living form, and exhibited that mastery of and delight in the horse that was such a feature of his work. Disconcerted by the tempest of contradictory opinion which arose over these two pictures, Géricault gave way to his enthusiasm for horses and soldiers and enrolled in the *mousquetaires*. During the Hundred Days he followed the king to Béthune, but, on his regiment being disbanded, he eagerly returned to his profession. He left France for Italy in 1816, and in Rome nobly depicted his favourite animal in his great painting *Free Horses racing in Rome*. Returning to Paris, Géricault exhibited *The Raft of the Medusa* (Louvre) at the Salon of 1819. This subject not only enabled him to prove his zealous and scientific study of the human form, but contained those elements of the heroic and pathetic that existed in modern life, to which he had appealed in his earliest productions.

Easily depressed or elated, Géricault took the hostility that this work excited to heart, and went on to spend nearly two years in London, where *The Raft of the Medusa* was exhibited with success, and where he executed many series of admirable lithographs, now rare. At the end of 1822 he was again in Paris, and produced a great quantity of projects for vast compositions, models in wax, and a flayed horse as a preliminary to an equestrian statue. His health was by then in decline due to various excesses, and on the 26th January 1824 he died at the age of thirty-three.

Théodore Géricault, *The Wounded Cuirassier,* 1814.
Oil on canvas, 358 x 294 cm. Musée du Louvre, Paris.

Théodore Géricault,
The Raft of the Medusa, 1819.
Oil on canvas, 491 x 716 cm.
Musée du Louvre, Paris.

Ary Scheffer, *The Dead Go Quickly,* 1820-1830.
Oil on canvas, 59 x 76 cm. Musée des Beaux-Arts, Lille.

Ary Scheffer, *Orpheus and Eurydice.*
Oil on canvas, 160 x 128 cm. Château de Blois, Blois.

Arie Scheffer, called **Ary Scheffer**
(Dort, 1795 – Argenteuil, 1858)

A French painter of Dutch extraction, Scheffer was born in Dort on the 10th February 1795. After the early death of his father, Ary was taken to Paris and placed in Guérin's studio by his mother, a woman of great energy and character. The end of Scheffer's time with Guérin coincided with the beginning of the Romantic movement. He had little sympathy with the directions taken by its most conspicuous representatives, Sigalon, Delacroix and Géricault, and made various tentative efforts – *Gaston de Foix* (1824), *Sulot Women* (1827) – before he found his own path. Immediately after the exhibition of the latter work he turned to Byron and Goethe, selecting from *Faust* a long series of subjects which had then an extraordinary vogue. Of these, we may mention *Margaret at her Wheel*, *Faust Doubting*, *Margaret on the Sabbath*, *Margaret Leaving Church*, the *Garden Walk*, and lastly, perhaps the most popular of all, *Margaret at the Well*. The two *Mignons* appeared in 1836, and *Francesca da Rimini*, which could be described as Scheffer's best work, belongs to the same period. He then turned to religious subjects: *Christus Consolator* (1836) was followed by *Christus Remunerator, The Shepherds led by the Star* (1837), *The Magi laying down their Crowns, Christ in the Garden of Gethsemane, Christ bearing his Cross, Christ Interred* (1845), *St Augustine and Monica* (1846), after which he ceased to exhibit his work, and, shut away in his studio, continued to produce paintings, many of which were only seen by the outside world only after his death in Argenteuil on 15th June 1858. At the posthumous exhibition of his works there figured the *Sorrows of the Earth* and the *Angel announcing the Resurrection*, which he had left unfinished. Amongst his numerous portraits those of La Fayette, Béranger, Lamartine and Marie-Amélie were the most noteworthy. His reputation, much shaken by this posthumous exhibition, was further undermined by the sale of the Paturle Gallery, which contained many of his most celebrated achievements; the charm and ease of their composition could not save them from the condemnation provoked by their poor and vapid sentiment. Scheffer, who married the widow of General Baudrand, was only made a Commander of the Legion of Honour in 1848 – that is, after he had wholly withdrawn from the Salon. His brother Henri, born in The Hague in 1798, was also a prolific painter.

Eugène Delacroix, *Hamlet before the Body of Polonius,* 1855.
Oil on canvas. Musée des Beaux-Arts, Reims.

Eugène Delacroix, *Dante and Virgil in Hell,* called *The Barque of Dante,* 1822.
Oil on canvas, 189 x 241 cm. Musée du Louvre, Paris.

Eugène Delacroix
(Saint-Maurice, 1798 – Paris, 1863)

Ferdinand Victor Eugène Delacroix (known as Eugène Delacroix) was one of the greatest colourists of the nineteenth century, in the sense of one who thinks and feels and expresses himself by means of colours and sees them in his mind's eye as a composition, before he begins to resolve the whole into its parts, and work out the separate details of form.

He nurtured his talent through the works of the colourists in the Louvre, especially Rubens. Indirectly it came out of the heart of the Romantic movement which had spread over Europe. Delacroix was inspired by the writers Goethe, Scott, Byron, and Victor Hugo. His own romantic nature flamed up through contact with theirs; he was possessed with their souls and became the first of the Romantic painters. He took many of his subjects from the poets of his preference, not to translate into literal illustrations, but to make them express in his own language of painting the most agitated emotions of the human heart.

On the other hand it is generally in the relationship of several figures, in other words in drama, that Delacroix finds the natural and striking expression of his ideas. His work is an immense and multiform poem, at once lyrical and dramatic, about passions – the violent and murderous passions which fascinate, dominate, and rend humanity. In the elaboration and execution of the pages of this poem, Delacroix does not forego any of his faculties as a man and an artist of vast intelligence standing on a level with the thoughts of the greatest in history, legend and poetry. Rather, he makes use of a feverish imagination always controlled by lucid reasoning and cool willpower. His expressive and life-like drawing, strong and subtle colour, sometimes composing a bitter harmony, sometimes overcast by that "sulphurous" note already observed by contemporaries, produce an atmosphere of storm, supplication, and anguish. Passion, movement and drama must not be supposed to engender disorder. With Delacroix as with Rubens, there hovers over the saddest representations, over tumults, horrors and massacre, a kind of serenity which is the sign of art itself and the mark of a mind that is master of its subject.

Richard Parkes Bonington, *Île de la Cité, Paris.*
Watercolour on paper vellum. Yale Center for British Art, New Haven.

Richard Parkes Bonington, *Rouen from the Quays,* 19th century.
The British Museum, London.

Richard Parkes Bonington
(Nottingham, 1802 – London, 1828)

Bonington was an influential English Romantic painter who typically produced landscape works. In 1817, his father's lace-making business took the family to Calais. Bonington had been taught English watercolour painting from a young age, and when the family moved to Paris in 1818 he met and became friends with Eugène Delacroix. In 1820 Bonington began to study at the École des beaux-arts, where he was taught by Gros. Following two years of exhibiting his works in the Paris Salon, he won a Gold Medal at the Salon of 1824. Between 1825 and 1827 he travelled to back and forth from London to Paris, and took a two-month trip to Switzerland and northern Italy with the artist Charles Rivet, where he made many sketches in oil and pencil. Bonington died of tuberculosis in London at the very young age of twenty-five.

Of Bonington's work, his friend Delacroix wrote in a letter to Théophile Thoré that "To my mind, one can find in other modern artists qualities of strength and of precision in rendering that are superior to those in Bonington's pictures, but no-one in this modern school, and perhaps even before, has possessed that lightness of touch which, especially in watercolors, makes his works a type of diamond which flatters and ravishes the eye, independently of any subject and any imitation." Bonington is frequently credited with having introduced English watercolour painting to the continent. His palette of cool blues contrasting with warmer orange and brown tones was typically English, as were his expansive washes of paint that gave a sense of space and light. His depictions of landscape and countryside were popular in travel books of the time, and he sketched furiously during his travels in Switzerland and Italy. Bonington truly mastered the watercolour technique, making the best use of both the medium and the subjects he chose, though he did also paint in oil. He was enormously influential, spreading awareness of developments in the watercolour medium and technique, and was celebrated by French artists and critics. Though little-known today, his style was hugely influential and much imitated during and after his time.

Théodore Chassériau, *Esther Preparing to Meet the King Ahasueras,* called *The Toilette of Esther,* 1841.
Oil on canvas, 45 x 35 cm. Musée du Louvre, Paris.

Théodore Chassériau, *The Tepidarium, "Room where the women of Pompeii came to rest and dry themselves after the bath"*, 1853. Oil on canvas, 171 x 258 cm. Musée d'Orsay, Paris.

Théodore Chassériau
(Sainte-Barbe-de-Samana, 1819 – Paris, 1856)

This French painter was born in what is now the Dominican Republic, though his family soon returned to Paris in 1821. His mother was the young Creole daughter of a landowner, and there has been speculation amongst historians as to how much Chassériau's mixed-race background affected his life and work. He was a well-known painter of portraits and historical pieces, his *Tepidarium at Pompeii* (1853) being now in the Musée d'Orsay. He studied under Ingres in Paris at the very young age of eleven, indicating that he was something of a child prodigy, and in 1840 travelled to Rome with his master, subsequently falling under the influence of Eugène Delacroix. He soon began to be influenced by Romanticism and developed a style that united Ingres' precision with Delacroix' rich, exotic colours. When he exhibited in the Salon of 1836, Chassériau took the third-place medal at the age of just seventeen years.

One of Chassériau's most important commissions was a fresco cycle in the Palais d'Orsay in 1844, then the Cour des Comptes. This consisted of fifteen decorative panels covering 269.4 square metres, including six large allegorical scenes. The central themes were Force and Order, which led to Peace, which in turn led to international trade, the last embodied by one of the panels depicting *Eastern Merchants on a Western Shore*. The building was destroyed in a fire during the Paris Commune of 1871, and the frescos were left open to the elements until the artist's family and friends pushed for them to be rescued and restored in 1891, just before the Palais d'Orsay itself was knocked down to make way for the Gare d'Orsay. Fragments of the frescos were preserved on canvas in the stores of the Louvre, but were again damaged by floods in 1910. They remain in the Louvre, having been restored twice since.

Chassériau's travels in Algeria in 1846 had a huge influence on his later work, inspiring elements of Orientalism that themselves influenced other painters. He died after a period of ill-health at the age of thirty-seven.

François Rude, *Head of the Marseillaise.*
Painted plaster, 41 x 29 x 29 cm. Musée du Louvre, Paris.

François Rude, *Departure of the Volunteers of 1792*, called *La Marseillaise,* 1832-1836.
Stone. 1160 x 600 cm. Arc de Triomphe, Paris.

François Rude
(Dijon, 1784 – Paris, 1855)

The French sculptor François Rude, the son of a locksmith, received only the most elementary instruction and was not able to attend the Dijon Free School of Drawing, Painting, and Modelling. After several difficult years of manual labour, he decided in 1807 to move to Paris. The superintendent of fine arts, Baron Denon, having seen Rude's statuette of *Theseus picking up a Discus*, which he had brought from Dijon, recommended him as an assistant to the sculptor Gaulle, commissioned to do a section of a *bas-relief* for the restoration of the *Column of the Grand Army*. Rude assisted Gaulle with the execution of this commission and was admitted at the same time as a student of Cartellier. In 1812 he received the Prix de Rome for a *bas-relief* of *Le Berger Aristée pleurant la Perte de ses Abeilles* (*Berger Aristée weeping for the Loss of his Bees*), which he destroyed himself in 1843. Financial difficulties postponed his departure for Italy. During the Hundred Days, Rude joined the Bonapartist movement in his home-town. After his benefactor had been forced to flee following the restoration of the Bourbons, Rude had to leave for Brussels, where he became known as a sculptor and opened a school. In 1827, following the advice of the painter Gros and the sculptors Cartellier and Roman, he returned to Paris. In 1828 he unveiled an *Immaculate Virgin* at the Salon, created in plaster and commissioned by the Saint-Gervais church, as well as the model of *Mercury attaching his Winged Sandals*. Between 1833 and 1835 he created the *Departure of the Volunteers of 1792*, a high relief on the Arc de Triomphe, one of the most celebrated pieces of modern French Art.

Rude presented himself before the Institute four times without success. In 1855 his name was entered on the jury list for prizes at the World Fair, and his peers awarded him the first medal of honour of the section. The great sculptor enjoyed as much respect for the dignity of his character as he did for his talent as an artist.

David d'Angers, *Monument to the Memory of Charles-Artus de Bonchamps (1759-1793),* 1825.
Plaster, 140 x 257 cm. Musée des Beaux-Arts, Angers.

David d'Angers, *Johann Wolfgang von Goëthe,* 1829.
Plaster, 83 x 58 x 51 cm. Musée d'Orsay, Paris.

Pierre Jean David, called David d'Angers
(Angers, 1788 – Paris, 1856)

Usually called David d'Angers, this French sculptor was born at Angers on the 12th March 1789. His father was also a sculptor, but he had thrown aside his mallet and taken up the musket, fighting against the Chouans of La Vendée. He returned to his trade at the end of the civil war to find his customers gone, so that young David was born into poverty. As the boy grew up his father hoped to force him into some more lucrative and certain way of life, but David was drawn to sculpture. He eventually succeeded in overcoming this opposition to his desire to become a sculptor, and at the age of eighteen left for Paris to study the art with a capital of eleven francs. After struggling against want for a year and a half, he succeeded in taking the prize at the École des beaux-arts. An annuity of 600 francs (£24) was granted by the municipality of his native town in 1809, and in 1811 David's *Epaminondas* gained the *Prix de Rome*. He spent five years in Rome.

Returning from Rome around the time of the Restoration of the Bourbons, he did not remain in the neighbourhood of the Tuileries, which swarmed with foreign conquerors and returned royalists, and instead went to London. Here Flaxman and others berated him for the sins of David the painter, to whom he was erroneously supposed to be related. With great difficulty he made his way back to Paris, where a comparatively prosperous career opened up to him. His medallions and busts were much in demand, and he was also given commissions for monumental works. One of the best of these was that of Gutenberg in Strasbourg, but those he himself valued most were the statue of Barra, a drummer boy who continued to beat his drum until the moment of death in the war in La Vendée, and the mausoleum of the Greek liberator Botzaris, consisting in a young female figure called *Reviving Greece*, of which Victor Hugo said, "It is difficult to see anything more beautiful in the world; this statue joins the grandeur of Pheidias to the expressive manner of Puget." David's busts and medallions were numerous, and among his sitters could be found not only the illustrious men and women of France, but many others both of England and Germany, countries which he visited in his professional capacity in 1827 and 1829. His medallions, it is affirmed, number some five hundred. An example of his benevolence of character can be found in his rushing off to the sick-bed of Rouget de Lisle, the author of *La Marseillaise*, modelling and carving him in marble without delay, making a lottery of the work, and sending the needy poet the seventy-two *livres* that resulted from the sale. David died on the 4th January 1856. His fame rests firmly on his pediment of the Panthéon, his monument to General Gobert in Père Lachaise and his marble *Philopoemen* in the Louvre. In the Musée David d'Angers is an almost complete collection of his works either originals or in the form of copies.

James Pradier, *Nyssia,* 1848.
Marble, h. : 176 cm. Musée Fabre, Montpellier.

James Pradier, *Satyr and Bacchante,* 1834.
Marble, h. : 125 cm. Musée du Louvre, Paris.

Jean-Jacques Pradier, called James Pradier
(Geneva, 1790 – Bougival, 1852)

The Swiss-born French sculptor, James Pradier, was a member of the French Academy, and a popular sculptor of the pre-Romantic period, representing in France the drawing-room Classicism which Canova illustrated in Rome. He was born in Geneva, but at the age of seventeen left for Paris, where his brother worked as an engraver. In 1813 he won the Prix de Rome, and so departed for Italy.

After spending four years in Rome, from 1814 to 1818, he studied with Ingres in Paris, and soon became a friend of the Romantic poets Alfred de Musset, Victor Hugo and Théophile Gautier. His studio became a meeting-place for Romantic thinkers, presided over by his mistress Juliette Drouet, who was the model for Pradier's statue representing *Strasbourg* in the Place de la Concorde. Between 1871 and 1918, when the region of Alsace-Lorraine was lost to Germany, this statue was frequently draped in mourning crêpe and decorated with wreaths. It is a typical example of Pradier's sensual classical sculptures of women. His works, showing neo-Classical influence, are filled with an eroticism that made his *Satyr and Bacchante* the centre of a scandal during the Salon in 1834. Louis-Philippe's government refused the work, which was eventually sold to Count Anatole Demidoff and taken to his palazzo in Florence, though it was later returned to Paris. Louis-Philippe was a great admirer of Pradier's work, though the sculptor was famously apolitical, and adapted to the regime of the time. He also provided official works such as figures for the Arc de Triomphe, the church of the Madeleine and les Invalides.

His work, very famous in his time, has now been largely forgotten. However, in 1846 Gustave Flaubert wrote: "This is a great artist, a true Greek, the most antique of all the moderns."

Antoine-Louis Barye, *Lion and Snake,* 1833.
Bronze, 135 x 178 x 96 cm. Musée du Louvre, Paris.

Antoine-Louis Barye, *Python Killing a Gnu,* 1834-1835.
Plaster and red wax, 27.9 x 39 cm. J. Paul Getty Museum, Los Angeles.

Antoine-Louis Barye
(Paris, 1796-1875)

Barye was a French sculptor, born in Paris on the 24th September 1796. As did many of the Renaissance sculptors, he began life as a goldsmith. After studying under Bosio, the sculptor, and Gros, the painter, he was admitted to the École des beaux-arts in 1818. But it was not until 1823, when he was working for Fauconnier, the goldsmith, that he discovered his real vocation through watching wild beasts in the Jardin des Plantes, making vigorous studies of them in pencil drawings worthy of Delacroix and then modelling them in sculpture on a large or small scale. In 1831 he exhibited his *Tiger devouring a Gharial*, and in 1832 had mastered a style of his own in the *Lion with a Snake*. Thenceforward Barye, though engaged in a perpetual struggle with poverty, exhibited year after year these studies of animals – admirable groups which reveal him to have been inspired by a spirit of true romance and a feeling for the beauty of the antique, as in *Theseus fighting the Minotaur* (1847), *Lapitha and Centaur* (1848), and numerous minor works now very highly valued.

Barye was no less successful in sculpture on a small scale, and excelled in representing animals in their most familiar attitudes. As examples of his larger work we may mention the *Lion of the Column of July*, the plaster model of which was cast in 1839, various lions and tigers in the gardens of the Tuileries, and the four groups – *War, Peace, Strength* and *Order* (1854). In 1852 he cast his bronze *Jaguar devouring a Hare*. The fame he deserved came too late to the sculptor. He was made professor of the museum in 1854, and was elected to the Academy of Fine Arts in 1868. He died on the 25th June 1875. The mass of admirable work left to us by Barye entitles him to be regarded as the greatest artist of animal life of the French school, and as the creator of a new class of art which has attracted such men as Frémiet, Peter, Cain, and Gardet, who are regarded with justice as his worthiest followers.

Jean-Étienne Chaponnière, *David Gives Thanks to God for his Victory over Goliath,* 1834.
Plaster, h. : c. 86 cm. Musée d'art et d'histoire, Geneva.

Jean-Étienne Chaponnière
(Geneva, 1801 – Mornex, 1835)

Born in Geneva, Chaponnière studied drawing with the Société des Arts, before learning engraving under Joseph Collart and Charles Wielandy. He studied in Paris from 1822, later as a student of the Swiss sculptor James Pradier. In the late 1820s he travelled in Italy, staying in Naples, Florence and Rome. Whilst in Naples he had his first masterpiece, *Young Captive Girl crying on Byron's Tomb* (1827), sent back to Geneva. The Philhellenists of Geneva acquired the work for the Musée Rath, which allowed him to become an honorary member of the Société des Arts. An allegorical *bas-relief,* ordered by the Société des Arts and entitled *Son of Tell* for the bust of the physicist Marc-Auguste Pictet, was then sent by Chaponnière from Naples to Berne, as well as a group named *Hunting and Fishing,* both of which were successfully exhibited in Geneva in 1829. After a brief stay in his home country, Chaponnière moved to Paris. The group sculpture *Hunting and Fishing* was exhibited in 1831 under the title *Daphnis and Chloe,* and was admired for its "naïveté". *Young Captive Girl crying on Byron's Tomb* was renamed *A Captive Girl from Missolonghi* and shown in the Salon of 1833, at the same time as four portrait-statuettes that were hailed by the Parisian critics as the invention of a new genre. In 1834 Chaponnière submitted to the Salon his model of a *bas-relief* destined for the Arc de Triomphe, *General Kléber taking Alexandria,* which was much admired. Other commissions followed, but the artist's health was is decline. *David, Victor over Goliath* was his final masterpiece, and was a runaway success at the Salon of 1835. It was cast in bronze for the Promenade des Bastions in Geneva almost twenty years later. Despite his brief life and career, Chaponnière produced some important examples of Romantic sculpture.

Jean-Étienne Chaponnière, *Young Greek Mourning at Byron's Tomb,* 1827.
Plaster, h. : 94 cm. Musée d'art et d'histoire, Geneva.

Auguste Préault, *Silence,* 19th century.
Bronze. Musée-Abbaye Saint-Germain, Auxerre.

Auguste Préault, *Ophelia,* 1876.
Bronze, 75 x 200 x 20 cm. Musée d'Orsay, Paris.

Antoine Augustin Préault, called Auguste Préault
(Paris, 1809-1879)

A student under the neo-Classical sculptor David d'Angers, Auguste Préault first exhibited two *bas-reliefs* at the Salon in 1833. Of a violent nature, these works were immediately hailed by the Romantics. However, the work undertaken during the revolutions of July 1830 was not well accepted in the art world. Over several years, Préault was completely rejected by the official exhibitions' network, whose doors would not open again for him until 1839. His return was largely celebrated, notably by the critic Théophile Gautier: "Regarding Préault, he is a sculptor full of life and movement, audacious, and following his idea until the end, a man of energy who understands statue making in a great manner and who, after a most brilliant beginning, has seen the doors of the Salon closed to him for five or six years..." Attracted by pathetic subjects, lending themselves perfectly to the Romantic treatment which allows translation of emotions with emphasis, Préault's style is characterised by incomparable vigour and warmth. Inspired by the works of Shakespeare, in 1842 he started working on a representation of Ophelia, who drowned herself after being rejected by Hamlet. Préault represented the depth of the stream, the hair swirling in the fleetingness of the moment which carries her away forever. Refused by the Salon of 1849, the *bas-relief* in plaster was exhibited the following year and the work was cast in bronze by order of the state in 1876. A sincere artist with an instinct for drama, staying close to the convictions of his youth, Auguste Préault died in Paris in 1879.

Jean-Baptiste Carpeaux, *The Triumph of Flora*, 1866.
Plaster, h. : 151 cm. Musée d'Orsay, Paris.

Jean-Baptiste Carpeaux, *The Dance*, 1868.
Stone, 420 x 297 x 196 cm. Musée d'Orsay, Paris.

Jean-Baptiste Carpeaux
(Valenciennes, 1827 – Courbevoie, 1875)

The French sculptor Jean-Baptiste Carpeaux was the son a stonemason, and his family lived in great poverty. At the age of fifteen he moved to Paris, and two years later he was admitted to the École des beaux-arts. He executed the much admired statue of *Hector and Astyanax* for which he was awarded the Prix de Rome in 1854. Disagreeing with the French Academy and fascinated by the works of Michelangelo and Donatello, he decided to move to Rome in 1856. There he created, amongst others, his masterpiece *Ugolino*, a dramatic group based on Dante's *Inferno*. Although it gained him only a second class medal at the Salon, it was admired by Napoleon and the court, assuring him permanent success as well as notoriety. The imperial prince commissioned a statue from Carpeaux. Among other famous works, he decorated the Pavillon de Flore and designed the frontispiece of the town hall of Valenciennes. In 1869 the group he made for the Opéra Garnier, *The Dance*, created a scandal with its freedom of movement and laughing characters. Another of his later masterpieces was the Parisian fountain, *The Four Quarters of the World*, featuring a globe which is held by four female forms representing the four continents. Carpeaux received many honours during his life. His best sculptures are noble in conception, his style naturalistic and full of emotion.

Jean-Baptiste Carpeaux, *Mater Dolorosa,* 1869-1870.
Terra cotta, 71.1 x 52.7 x 34.8 cm. Musée des Beaux-Arts, Valenciennes.

Jean-Baptiste Carpeaux, *Ugolino,* 1862.
Bronze, 194 x 148 x 119 cm. Musée d'Orsay, Paris.

Bibliography

Abercrombie, Lascelles, *Romanticism*, London, M. Secker, 1927

Alexander, Vera, *Romantik*, Trier, WVT, 2000

Bietak, Wilhelm, *Lebenslehre und weltanschauung der jüngeren romantic*, Leipzig, P. Reclam jun., 1936

Bony, Jacques and Bergez, Daniel, *Lire le Romantisme*, Paris, Dunod, 1992

Brown, Marshall, *The Cambridge history of literary criticism. Volume 5, Romanticism*, Cambridge, Cambridge University Press, 2000

Collective work, *Le Romantisme allemand*, Paris, H. Champion, 1978

Focillon, Henri and Loyrette, Henri, *La Peinture au XIXe siècle*, Paris, Flammarion, 1991

Huch, Ricarda, *Blütezeit der Romantik*, Leipzig, G. Haeffel, 1913

Ormesson, Jean (d'), *Une Autre Histoire de la littérature française*, Paris, Éd. J'ai lu, 2000

Ruston, Sharon, *Romanticism*, London, New York, Continuum, 2007

Usami, Hitoshi, *Romantisme français*, Kyoto, Rinsen Books, 1993

Index